The Incomparable Friend

The Life of Bahá'u'lláh Told in Stories

"More and more people came to respect and love Baha'u'llah. …… Once, when He was walking to Mírzá Músá's house, He passed a coffee shop where the new officer in charge of customs was sitting with his assistants. To their own surprise the officer and all his assistants found themselves rising to their feet and bowing to Him. He greeted them lovingly and passed on. The officer turned in bewilderment to his friends and asked, 'Is this the Holy Spirit or the King of Kings? Who is He?'"

Who is He?

Using stories, this book describes events in the life of Bahá'u'lláh, the Founder of the Bahá'í Faith. From these stories you may build a picture in your mind of who He was.

How did the people around Him feel when they were with Bahá'u'lláh? These true-to-life stories give an inkling of why He was called the 'Incomparable Friend'.

The Incomparable Friend

The Life of Bahá'u'lláh Told in Stories

Shirin Sabri

paintings by Sue Podger

Bahá'í Publications Australia

& Ilxir Publications Inc.

The Incomparable Friend

© Text Shirin Sabri 2006
© Paintings Sue Podger 2006

© Copyright 2006
First eBook version 2017
First POD version 2019

Bahá'í Publications Australia
&
Ilxir Publications Inc.

All Rights Reserved
Copyright under Berne Convention

Original Book Design & Layout: Massoud Tahzib
Updated Design for POD: Bahá'í Publications Australia

For Faraz, Amelia and Omid,
the first readers and critics of this book

Table of Contents

Introduction ix

Chapter:

1	Birth and Childhood	1
2	The Puppet Show	5
3	A Prayer for Peace	9
4	Mírzá Buzurg's Dream	13
5	Bahá'u'lláh's Marriage to Navváb	17
6	Bahá'u'lláh receives the Writings of the Báb	23
7	Bahá'u'lláh rescues Ṭáhirih	29
8	The Conference at Badasht	35
9	The Attack at Níyálá	41
10	The Visit to Fort Ṭabarsí	47
11	Bahá'u'lláh's letter to the Báb and His Reply	53
12	The Visit to Karbilá	57
13	The Attempt on the Life of the Sháh	61
14	The Síyáh-Chál	67
15	Release from the Síyáh-Chál	71
16	The Journey to Baghdád	79
17	Baghdád	85
18	Bahá'u'lláh's Life in the Wilderness	89
19	Life in Baghdád	95
20	Departure from Baghdád	101

21	Constantinople	109
22	Adrianople	115
23	The Poisoning	121
24	The Tablets to the Kings	125
25	Adrianople – The Last Years	131
26	The Journey to Akká	137
27	The Most Great Prison	143
28	The Death of Mírzá Mihdí	149
29	In the City	153
30	Mazra'ih and Bahjí	159
31	The Death of Navváb	165
32	The Last Days	171
33	The Passing of Bahá'u'lláh	175
34	The Covenant	179
35	Bahá'u'lláh's Resting Place	183

Glossary 188

Some Important Dates 191

References 194

Bibliography 198

A Guide to Pronunciation 199

Tihrán, where Bahá'u'lláh was born

Introduction

In the middle of the Nineteenth Century, when the events narrated here occurred, the world was in a state of expectation. Many people saw that great changes were needed to make life more just and more peaceful for all who live on earth. Some had begun to dream of a world without war, and others, in both the East and the West, had decided that a new Messenger from God must be about to appear.

In the Christian West, the members of some churches prepared for the return of Christ and the end of the world. In the Muslim East, a group of young men began a remarkable search. They set out to find the Messenger of God, looking for him, as the prophecies of Islám taught them, in the towns of Persia. They understood that he would be living, just as Jesus and Muḥammad did, among the ordinary people of their time, teaching a new way of life.

These young men found the One they were looking for. He was living in the city of Shíráz. He told them that his title was the 'Báb'. This title means the 'Gate', and the Báb explained that he had come to open the way to one far greater than himself. He announced that he had come to prepare the way for the Promised One of all ages and all peoples, the One who would bring peace to the world at last.

The Promised One whose coming the Báb announced was Bahá'u'lláh, whose title means the 'Glory of God'. This book tells the story of Bahá'u'lláh's life from his childhood and early years as a nobleman in Ṭihrán, to the insecure existence of a prisoner and exile far from home. His was a life of great suffering, but throughout it he taught his followers to love humanity and to work tirelessly to build a world without prejudice, hatred or war. He was the true and incomparable friend of all mankind.

The stories in this book bring us directly in touch with the selfless life Bahá'u'lláh chose to lead. At the same time, they help us understand better the great and never-ending Covenant of love between God and mankind.

Birth and Childhood

One morning as the sun rose over Ṭihrán, a Child was born.

One morning as the sun rose over Ṭihrán, a Child was born. He was born into a family that was powerful in the government of Persia, and was also rich. The house where he was born looked more like a palace than a house, with its tall columned walkways and arched windows looking out over the walled garden.

This child was very special, right from the start. He never cried or fussed in the way that little babies ordinarily do, which surprised his mother very much. People used to shake their heads and say, 'Such a child will not live', because they felt he was too good for this world. His name was Mírzá Ḥusayn 'Alí, but he will always be known as Bahá'u'lláh.

The house where Bahá'u'lláh was born

Bahá'u'lláh never went to school at all, though of course he was taught the things that noble boys usually learnt, like horse riding, sword fighting and to shoot a gun. He would have read poetry and the *Qur'án*, and also have learnt to write, but that was all. The odd thing was that even though he had not been taught things like history and philosophy, he knew it all anyway. Grown-ups were often very surprised to find that he knew more than they did!

Once, when he was visiting a famous scholar, who was like a professor at a college, he sat up in the evening and listened while the scholar questioned his students. The scholar asked the students to explain the meaning of a Muslim tradition, but none of them could do it. Out of politeness, he then asked Bahá'u'lláh to try. Bahá'u'lláh quietly gave such a clear explanation of the tradition that nobody else could think of anything to say, they were so astonished. The next day the great scholar was very angry with his students. 'I have taught you for twenty-five years', he shouted, 'and yet this youth knows more than you do!'

Bahá'u'lláh loved the outdoors, and the fresh beauty of the countryside. He spent much of his time out in the garden or riding on horseback through the hills around his family's country house.

One day, when his family was staying at this country house, he saw a government tax collector bullying his father and being very rude. This tax collector was trying to make Bahá'u'lláh's father, Mírzá Buzurg, pay all sorts of taxes that he didn't even owe. Bahá'u'lláh knew that this was unjust. He couldn't bear to see his father treated so badly, so he decided to do something about it. He took his horse and rode for two whole days until he came to Ṭihrán. He told the people in the government what the tax collector was doing, and made them see how wrong it was. They agreed that such a dishonest bully should not keep his job. Then Bahá'u'lláh took the papers ordering the tax collector to leave his job straight away, and rode back to his parents.

The Puppet Show

When Bahá'u'lláh was a young child he was taken to the celebrations for his elder brother's wedding.

W hen Bahá'u'lláh was a young child he was taken to the celebrations for his elder brother's wedding. The feasts and banquets for this wedding went on for seven days, because that was the way weddings were celebrated among the nobles of that time in Persia. On the last day, all the guests were invited to a puppet show called 'The Show of Sultán Salím'.

The audience settled down to watch. The curtain rose, and little figures only a few inches tall marched out of a grand tent on the stage, shouting, 'The King is coming, arrange the seats in order.' Then more little figures came out and

6

Puppet show of the King and his court watching an execution

busily swept the ground, while others sprinkled water on the streets to settle the dust. Now the herald appeared, and announced the King.

A great procession came out onto the stage. First came the government ministers with their hats and shawls, then attendants, officials, guards and an executioner with his axe. All these puppets lined up, looking astonishingly life-like. They bowed low to the King as he walked slowly and majestically past them to seat himself upon his throne. He looked about at his subjects gravely, his jeweled crown glittering in the stage lights.

At that moment guns fired a salute and the national anthem rang out. Smoke from the guns swirled around the puppets and slowly cleared. When it had gone the audience saw that all the ministers, attendants and various officials had lined up before the King, their place in line depending on how important they were.

Now a thief was dragged in by the police, and brought before the King for judgment. The King ordered that he should be beheaded. The executioner came forward and chopped off his head, and it looked as if real blood was trickling from the puppet-prisoner's severed head.

The King turned away and began consulting with his ministers about matters of state. Then messengers rushed in, announcing that a rebellion had started. The puppet-King ordered his soldiers to march out and put a stop to it. Soon the thunder of heavy artillery echoed from behind the stage. Bahá'u'lláh gazed at the wondrous spectacle in amazement.

At last the curtain fell, and the puppet show was finished. A while later, Bahá'u'lláh saw a man come out from behind the stage, carrying a wooden box under his arm.
'What is in that box?' Bahá'u'lláh asked him, 'Where is the King and all the men?'
'He is folded up in this box, with all his finery, and so are all the rest of them', answered the puppeteer.

At that moment Bahá'u'lláh clearly saw that a real king and all his ministers were exactly the same as those little puppets. They too would parade in splendour for a short while on the earth, and then would be folded away in a wooden box under the ground.

He saw that all the wealth and treasures that the nobles possessed, all the beautiful robes and jewels that they owned and all the brave soldiers under their command meant absolutely nothing. From that time on, Bahá'u'lláh had no thought for the things of this world. He saw that all the struggles for power and wealth that people spent their lives on were truly no more important than the puppet show. Even though he was only a young child at that time, he decided that from then on he would only care about what God wanted, for he saw that nothing else truly mattered.

A Prayer for Peace

When we read about the extraordinary things that Bahá'u'lláh was able to do, even as a child, we can see that he was not an ordinary person.

Whhen we read about the extraordinary things that Bahá'u'lláh was able to do, even as a child, we can see that he was not an ordinary person. People who knew him as a child or youth realised that he was gifted, even though they could not know what the future would hold for him.

Until the time is right for a Messenger of God to receive a Revelation from Him, the truth about the Messenger's spiritual nature is hidden. If we think of the Messenger as a perfect mirror, able to reflect all of God's qualities, then we can imagine that in his childhood, that perfect mirror is wrapped in protective veils. People glimpse flashes of something wonderful, but they do not know what it might be.

A page from an early Qur'án, verses 79 and 80 of the Surat An'Nisa, in the Kufic script. The text begins: "Whatever good, (O man!) happens to thee, is from God, but whatever evil happens to thee, is from thine own soul."

'Abdu'l-Bahá, the eldest son of Bahá'u'lláh, explains it like this:
Before declaring Their manifestation, They are silent and quiet, like a sleeper, and after Their manifestation, They speak and are illuminated, like one who is awake.

In this explanation of the nature of the Messengers of God, 'Abdu'l-Bahá uses capital letters for the words, 'Their' and 'They'. This is out of respect for the great station the Messenger occupies. Now, this is a story about the gradual lifting of the veils that began in Bahá'u'lláh's childhood. For this reason, beginning with the next story in this book, capital letters will be used as in 'He' and 'His', to refer to Bahá'u'lláh.

When Bahá'u'lláh was a child, he used to read the *Qur'án*, just as other boys of his age and background did. He also read poetry, and books about the history of Islám. He tells us that once, when he was reading, he came across the story of a tragic event in Islámic history, a massacre which happened in the early years of that Faith. As Bahá'u'lláh read of the bloodshed and the misery that had been caused, he was overcome by sorrow, grieving over the suffering that human beings cause each other.

Yet, at the same time, he remembered that God's mercy to humanity is endless. He knew that God would always forgive people for their mistakes, and would help them to do better. Turning to God, Bahá'u'lláh prayed.

He prayed, asking God to help the peoples of the world. He begged God to send something that would teach everyone how to live together in love and unity, so that terrible things like that massacre would not happen anymore.

Soon after this, a curious thing happened. One morning before dawn, Bahá'u'lláh tells us that he had an extraordinary feeling of being transformed. It affected his manners, his thoughts and his words. This strange process lasted for about twelve days. After that, he says, words surged from him as though they came from a mighty ocean, and the Sun of Assurance began to shine. He says that he continued in this state until the time when he received the Revelation in the Síyáh-Chál.

Although we cannot begin to understand what this was like, we do know, as 'Abdu'l-Bahá explained, that the Manifestation is always the Manifestation, even though that part of his nature is dormant, or sleeping, until the time is right. Perhaps we could say that at this moment in Bahá'u'lláh's childhood, the sleeper stirred, and began to dream of things to come.

Mírzá Buzurg's Dream

Bahá'u'lláh's father had begun to realise that his son was a very special Child.

Mírzá Buzurg's dream - the fishes holding onto Bahá'u'lláh's hair

Bahá'u'lláh's father had begun to realise that his son was a very special Child. Once, when His mother was watching Him as He paced thoughtfully beneath blossoming fruit trees in the garden, she remarked that He might be a little bit short. But His father exclaimed, 'That is not important! Look at His intelligence, see how perceptive He is! He is like a flame of fire. Even at this young age He outdoes grown men.'

Bahá'u'lláh's father dreamed a very strange dream about his son. In the dream, he saw Bahá'u'lláh swimming in the most enormous ocean. His body was shining, lighting up the ocean with a clear white light. His hair was floating out in all directions over the foaming waves. Then, in the dream, millions of fishes came, and each fish grabbed the end of one of Bahá'u'lláh's hairs, and held

14

it tight. Even though there were so many fish, and they were all holding on so tightly, not one of Bahá'u'lláh's hairs was torn out, and the fish did not bother Him at all. He swam freely through the water, and all the fish followed Him.

Mírzá Buzurg, Bahá'u'lláh's father, felt that such an unusual dream must be very important, so he called a famous soothsayer to explain it.

The soothsayer told Mírzá Buzurg that in the dream the ocean meant the world. He said that Bahá'u'lláh, all by Himself, would eventually rule over the whole world. He would go wherever He wished, and no one would be able to stop Him. He told Bahá'u'lláh's father that the fish were all the people who would gather round Bahá'u'lláh, and cling to Him. And he said that although

Bahá'u'lláh's father, Mírzá Buzurg

the things Bahá'u'lláh was going to have to do would stir up great storms and tempests in the world, and that He would be in great danger, the dream showed that He was under God's protection, and could never be harmed.

After hearing all this, Bahá'u'lláh's father was even more certain that his son had an amazing future ahead of him. He knew for certain now - this Son of his was no ordinary child.

Bahá'u'lláh's Marriage to Navváb

Bahá'u'lláh was only seventeen when He married Ásíyih Khánum, whom He called 'Navváb', and she was even younger.

17

Mules carrying the dowry of Bahá'u'lláh's wife, Navváb

Bahá'u'lláh was only seventeen when He married Ásíyih Khánum, whom He called 'Navváb', and she was even younger. Getting married while still very young was the custom among the Persians at that time. It took forty mules to bring all the treasures of her dowry to Bahá'u'lláh's house. Can you imagine? Forty mules, loaded with silks, furs, jewels and other precious things. For six whole months before the wedding a jeweller had worked at Navváb's home, making jewellery for her. Even the buttons on her clothes were made of gold

set with precious stones. Later on, Navváb would exchange the last of these buttons for a few pieces of bread, during the terrible winter journey in exile from Ṭihrán to Baghdád. But that is another story.

Navváb was lively and beautiful, a slender, graceful young noblewoman with gentle eyes of dark blue. Even though she was very young she was already known for her wisdom, intelligence and purity of heart.

From the very start of their marriage, Bahá'u'lláh and Navváb kept away from the grand occasions and ceremonies, which the nobles of Persia usually spent their time on. They both felt that these worldly pleasures had no meaning for them.

When their children 'Abbás Effendi (whom we know as 'Abdu'l-Bahá) and Fátimih (whom we know as Bahíyyih <u>Kh</u>ánum) were small, the family would go up into the mountains to stay at their country house. There the children

Bahá'u'lláh's country house in Tákur. The window opens into the room which His Son, 'Abbás Effendi, occupied when He was six.

would run and play among trees heavy with fruit and flowers, or lie dreaming by stone-edged pools watching the gliding shadows of fish slide by beneath green water. This was the time of peace and happiness, and it seemed that nothing could disturb the smoothly flowing days.

Mostly Bahá'u'lláh and Navváb spent their time caring for the poor, giving help and comfort to those who were in trouble. The people called Bahá'u'lláh the 'Father of the Poor' and they spoke of Navváb as the 'Mother of Consolation' -

though of course only the women and children ever saw her face. The kindness of Bahá'u'lláh and His wife amazed the people. They were used to nobles who were full of their own pride, and bullied ordinary people without even thinking about it. In those days the nobles of Persia only cared about their own pleasures. They would never have dreamt of letting ordinary poor people troop into their houses, let alone of giving them food and medicine and money the way that Bahá'u'lláh and Navváb did.

Bahá'u'lláh was so generous that His friends were afraid He would soon give away everything He had. He didn't try to get Himself an important position in the government, either, which really surprised the other nobles. 'Why is it that such an intelligent young Man doesn't look for a chance to be important? Why doesn't He spend His life as we do? Think how much money He could make if He did!' 'Why doesn't He think of Himself?' they asked each other.

But some who were wiser answered, 'He is connected to another world. He will do some great thing one day; we just have to wait and see what it will be.'

Bahá'u'lláh Receives the Writings of the Báb

One day the Bab called Mulla Husayn, the first to believe in Him, to His presence.

One day the Báb called Mullá Ḥusayn, the first to believe in Him, to His presence. 'I have a very important mission for you', He said, about three months after He had declared Himself to be a Messenger of God. 'Take this Tablet. You must deliver it to a great and holy person.'
'But who is he? And how shall I find him?' asked Mullá Ḥusayn in surprise. Then the Báb told him first to go to Ṭihrán, and then to look for a nobleman who was known to be very spiritual, and always kind to the poor. He told Mullá Ḥusayn some other special things to look for too, so that he would be sure that he had found the right person.

Mullá Ḥusayn went to Ṭihrán, and stayed at a place of learning, like a college or university, where people studied the *Qur'án* and the traditions of Islám. The first thing he did was to speak to the head teacher of that college - after all, he ought to have been a spiritual person! But the head teacher became angry when Mullá Ḥusayn tried to tell him about the Báb. He argued and shouted and wouldn't let Mullá Ḥusayn finish what he wanted to say.

Unnoticed by either of them, a humble young student named Mullá Muḥammad had overheard the whole exchange. This student listened to every word Mullá Ḥusayn managed to say, and he knew in his heart that it was all true. He couldn't understand why his learned teacher was arguing against the truth. He kept very quiet, and thought hard about what had happened.

The Shikastih-nasta'liq script in which Bahá'u'lláh excelled

That night, at midnight, Mullá Muḥammad crept up to Mullá Ḥusayn's door, and softly knocked. Mullá Ḥusayn was still awake, and asked him in. 'I am so sorry about the way my teacher has treated you!' exclaimed Mullá Muḥammad. 'I know that you have brought us a great truth - I cannot understand why he would not listen.'

Mullá Ḥusayn gave a great sigh of relief. 'Now I see why it was that I felt I should stay here', he said. 'The head teacher rudely rejected my precious gift, but now his student has come to accept it!'

Tears rolled down Mullá Muḥammad's cheeks when he heard these words. Mullá Ḥusayn gently put his arms around the young man, then sat him down on a floor cushion and asked, 'Where are you from?'
'I am from Núr', answered Mullá Muḥammad.
'Do you know the family of Mírzá Buzurg, who recently died?'
'Why yes, of course I do', said the young man, a little puzzled by this question. Mullá Ḥusayn hesitated for a moment, thinking how to put his next question. 'Is there,' he asked, 'Is there anyone in that family who is known for his fine character and high intelligence?'
'Yes', replied Mullá Muḥammad slowly. 'One of Mírzá Buzurg's sons is well known for just those qualities.'
'What does he do?' asked Mullá Ḥusayn, leaning forward.

'He comforts those who are in trouble and feeds the hungry', came the reply.

Mullá Ḥusayn clapped his hands together. 'Does he hold any rank, or great position?' he asked next, gazing intently at the young man.
'No, he has none - except that the people call him the "Father of the Poor".'

Mullá Ḥusayn leaned back quietly.
'And what is his name?'
'Ḥusayn-'Alí.'
'And what kind of calligraphy does he write more beautifully than any other?'
'The <u>Sh</u>ikastih-nasta'líq script.'
'And how does he spend his time?'
'He roams through the woods, and loves the beauty of the countryside.'
Mullá Ḥusayn was smiling as he asked the last question, 'What is his age?'
'He is twenty-eight.'

Mullá Ḥusayn's eyes were glowing with excitement.
'Do you often meet him?'
'Yes', said the astonished student. 'I often go to his house.'
'Then will you take him this letter for me, and give it into his hands?'
'Of course I will', agreed Mullá Muḥammad, for he saw that this letter must be very important.

The next day he went to Bahá'u'lláh's house, and was taken in to see Him. He gave Bahá'u'lláh the Báb's letter. He opened it, and began to read, sometimes pausing to read parts of it aloud. Then He looked up, and said, 'Whoever believes in the *Qur'án* and knows that it is from God must also see that these Writings are from the same Source.'

He gave Mullá Muḥammad a gift of tea and Russian sugar for Mullá Ḥusayn. In those days tea and that kind of sugar were rare and expensive, and people often gave them as gifts - rather as we give chocolates today.

Filled with happiness, Mullá Muḥammad rushed back to Mullá Ḥusayn. He told Mullá Ḥusayn what Bahá'u'lláh had said, and gave him the gifts. Mullá Ḥusayn was overcome with joy. He took Bahá'u'lláh's gift with trembling hands, and kissed it. Then he kissed Mullá Muḥammad's eyes, because they had seen Bahá'u'lláh.

'Oh, my dear friend!' he exclaimed, wiping away tears. 'I hope that one day God will make you as happy as you have made me!'

Now Mullá Muḥammad really could not understand Mullá Ḥusayn's behaviour. Why should a simple gift from Bahá'u'lláh give him such happiness?

When he left Ṭihrán a few days later, Mullá Ḥusayn told Mullá Muḥammad, 'You must keep all this a secret. Do not talk to anyone about Him. Pray that God will protect Him, and assist Him to care for the weak and help the poor. The secret meaning of all this is hidden from you, but one day it will all become clear. For now, you must go out and teach everyone about the Báb, and spread His message.'

Mullá Muḥammad did as Mullá Ḥusayn told him, and one day much later on, he did understand the secret of that strange meeting.

Bahá'u'lláh Rescues Ṭáhirih

As word spread of the teachings of the Báb, many people in authority, such as government officials and religious leaders, became very angry.

29

As word spread of the teachings of the Báb, many people in authority, such as government officials and religious leaders, became very angry. They wanted the Báb to stop teaching so that He wouldn't gather any more followers. Three years after His Declaration He was imprisoned in the castle of Máh-Kú and many of the Bábís began to turn to Bahá'u'lláh for wise advice and help.

One day something terrible happened. An important religious leader was murdered, and people said that the Bábís had done it. This was not true and later on the real murderer confessed, and then everyone knew that an awful mistake had been made, but the people did not stop to think. They attacked the Bábís wherever they could find them, and many of the small band of believers were killed.

One of the Báb's first followers, known as the 'Letters of the Living', was the poet Ṭáhirih. She had been caught, and held captive in a house in Qazvín. But she was not afraid at all.

Bahá'u'lláh has arranged Ṭáhirih's escape

She stood before her captors with flashing eyes and declared, 'Before nine days have passed God will free me from your tyranny! If He does not free me before these nine days are up, you can do what you want with me, for you will have shown my belief to be false.'

After saying that you can imagine how closely watched Ṭáhirih was. Her captors were delighted, thinking that this was their chance to show her once and for all that the Bábí religion was not true.

Bahá'u'lláh was soon told about Ṭáhirih's extraordinary statement, and He straightaway said that she must be freed.
'But how shall we do it?' asked the other believers. 'Surely it is not possible? How could she have said such a thing?'

Bahá'u'lláh smiled gently and began to explain His plan. One of the Bábí women living in Qazvín, called K͟hátún-Ján, was to disguise herself as an old beggar woman. She would have a letter from Bahá'u'lláh hidden in her rags.

Then she would go to the house where Ṭáhirih was held captive and beg for alms. When she was allowed in, she would find Ṭáhirih and give her Bahá'u'lláh's letter explaining what to do, and letting her know that Khátún-Ján could be trusted. Then Khátún-Ján was to go and wait just outside the house until Ṭáhirih could come out to her.

Khátún-Ján did all this, exactly as Bahá'u'lláh said, although she couldn't quite see how Ṭáhirih was to get out of the house with all those people watching her. But strangely enough, that was the easiest part of the whole thing. Somehow Ṭáhirih was able to walk right out of the house without anyone seeing her, and soon she was standing beside Khátún-Ján in the street, all covered in her veil. As soon as she was veiled no one could see who she was, or pick out two veiled ladies walking by from all the others in the street, because they all looked the just the same - like black tents, drifting past.

The two ladies walked quickly to Khátún-Ján's house, where her husband, Áqá Hádí, and an attendant named Áqá Qulí, who was not a believer, were waiting with the three swift horses Bahá'u'lláh had sent. As soon as night came they mounted the horses and rode for Ṭihrán, straight to Bahá'u'lláh's house. By the time the nine days were up Ṭáhirih was safe with Navváb, and under Bahá'u'lláh's protection.

The day after arriving at Bahá'u'lláh's house, Ṭáhirih and Áqá Hádí went on to stay in a nearby village. The next day Bahá'u'lláh and Áqá Qulí, the attendant, followed them. Before they left for the village, Bahá'u'lláh asked Áqá Qulí to pack a heap of gold and silver coins into a saddle bag. He told Áqá Qulí to pack the coins so that the gold coins were in one side and the silver ones in the other. But Áqá Qulí decided to pack the gold coins at the bottom of the bag, and the silver ones at the top. When Bahá'u'lláh saw the bag, He asked, 'Why did you do this? We told you to put the gold on one side and the silver on the other.'
'I did it', answered Áqá Qulí, 'for the simple reason that if some coins should fall when we load the bag onto the horse, or when we are riding along, the coins that fall out will be silver, and not gold.' Bahá'u'lláh said no more, and asked him to load the horses.

They rode out to the village where Ṭáhirih was staying, and that night all the guests stayed there. The next morning Ṭáhirih came to Áqá Qulí and told him that she had a feeling that he should go back to Qazvín, or great trouble would be caused. Bahá'u'lláh called Áqá Qulí, and said that He wished to give him money for his travelling expenses. He asked for the saddle bag to be brought. Then He told Áqá Qulí to hold out his coat, and dipped His hand nine times into the saddle bag, pouring the coins into Áqá Qulí's outspread coat. Áqá Qulí gazed down at the handfuls of coin piling up in his coat, and just for a moment found himself wishing that they had been gold. Bahá'u'lláh looked up at him with laughing eyes and said, 'We give you enough to take you to Qazvín. The money for your wedding feast will reach you later. In any case it is your own fault, you put the gold at the bottom!'

Áqá Qulí set off for Qazvín straight away, and when he arrived he found it was just as Ṭáhirih said. His family were already suspicious, and if he had come back any later they might have set out to find him - and then would have found Ṭáhirih. Soon after returning, he found himself a wealthy man, just as Bahá'u'lláh had promised him, and remained a friend of the Faith until he passed away.

Ṭáhirih knew very well who Bahá'u'lláh was - the poems she wrote show us that. It was because she understood the greatness of Bahá'u'lláh that she dared to challenge her captors in that bold way. She knew that Bahá'u'lláh would easily succeed in rescuing her from them, and that this rescue would become a way of teaching more people about the Báb.

Ṭáhirih's captors could not believe their eyes when they found that she had vanished. 'How could this have happened?' they cried. 'None of her friends came near this place! Who could have helped her?'

They searched high and low through Qazvín, but they could not find her. They could not explain what had happened, for they were all sure that Ṭáhirih had not been left alone for a moment. Indeed, some of the people of that household became Bábís because of Ṭáhirih's unexplainable escape.

The Conference at Badasht

After Ṭáhirih had stayed at Bahá'u'lláh's house for a while, He arranged for one of the believers to escort her to Badasht.

After Ṭáhirih had stayed at Bahá'u'lláh's house for a while, He arranged for one of the believers to escort her to Badasht. He Himself had preparations to make before setting off. Bábís from all over Persia were travelling to Badasht, because Bahá'u'lláh had asked them to come to a conference there.

When Bahá'u'lláh arrived He hired three walled gardens in Badasht. In those days it was quite usual for people to hire gardens when they wanted to stay somewhere. They would travel with their tents, and find a walled garden to hire wherever they wanted to stay. The gardens at Badasht were in a large field, so there was plenty of room for all the Bábís to set up their tents. Because Ṭáhirih was a woman, she had to be put in a garden by herself. So, one garden was for Ṭáhirih and her female companions, then the second one was for Bahá'u'lláh where there would be space for meetings. The third garden was for Quddús, another of the Letters of the Living, and some other Bábí men. Ṭáhirih would be allowed to come to meetings, but she would have to wear a veil covering her from head to toe, and she would have to sit apart from the men, behind a curtain.

Bahá'u'lláh had decided that it was time for the Bábís to let go of the Islámic laws and traditions that they were still clinging to - like making Ṭáhirih wear that veil. He knew that some of the Bábís were going to find these changes very frightening and difficult to accept. His way of teaching the Bábís the new laws was to let them see in a sudden and dramatic way that the old laws and customs needed to be thrown away. He knew that it would take a great shock to break the hold that these old ways had on them. He met with Ṭáhirih and Quddús, and the three of them discussed what they might do to bring about such a great change in the minds and hearts of the believers.

One day Bahá'u'lláh told all the Bábís that He was feeling ill, and had to remain in bed. As soon as Quddús heard, he went to visit Bahá'u'lláh, to see how He was. Quddús sat down beside the bed, and while he was talking with Bahá'u'lláh the other believers slowly came in. Of course, Ṭáhirih was not allowed in. She had to stay in her separate garden, not knowing what was going on and not able to be a part of it all.

After the believers had gathered in Bahá'u'lláh's tent, a messenger came from Ṭáhirih. He walked over to where Quddús was talking quietly with Bahá'u'lláh, and told Quddús that Ṭáhirih very much wanted him to come and see her in her garden. Bahá'u'lláh saw that the storm of change was building up. He lay back, and said nothing. At any time He could have stopped everyone in their tracks, only by saying a word. But He allowed the storm to build. It was going to work like a play, a play in which all the Bábís would come face to face with their own feelings and their own understanding of the new faith. This was the way they were going to learn the new laws, and understand that the Bábí Faith was truly a new religion with laws of its own, different from those of Islám.

Quddús straightened up and looked at Ṭáhirih's servant sternly. 'I will have nothing to do with her', he replied. 'Go and tell her that I will not come.' He was determined to remain with Bahá'u'lláh, to give Him any assistance He might need while He was ill.

The messenger stared at him in disbelief. How could he take such a rude message to Ṭáhirih? But Quddús glared at him so fiercely that he quickly backed out of the tent and went back to Ṭáhirih. The Bábís in the tent whispered together, wondering what was going to happen.

Then the messenger came back, with the same message as before. 'She says that she must speak with you. You must come!' he begged Quddús.
'I will not come', said Quddús, folding his arms.
'But, but sir!' pleaded the servant, wringing his hands. 'She says that if you do not come to her, she will come right in here to see you!'

The Bábís gasped. She could not do that! Islámic tradition forbade it!
'I will not come', repeated Quddús.

Then the servant unsheathed his sword, and gave it to Quddús with trembling hands. 'I cannot go back there without you', he said. 'Either you come with me now, or you take this sword and cut off my head!' And he knelt, with his neck stretched out.
'Very well, then', replied Quddús, standing up and lifting the sword above his head.

At that moment Ṭáhirih came into the tent. She walked in amongst the men without her veil. Quddús stared at her in shock, slowly lowering the sword.

The other Bábí men were horrified. How could Ṭáhirih, the Pure One, be doing such a disgraceful thing? They thought it was shameful if one of them even looked at her shadow accidentally, and now here she was, perfumed, wearing make-up and elegantly dressed, walking unveiled in front of them.

One of the men was so dismayed that he slashed at his throat and ran shrieking out of the tent covered in his own blood. You see, it seemed to them that Ṭáhirih had suddenly turned into a wicked person, because she was disobeying what they thought was a law of Islám. They had been used to thinking that she was the best and purest of women, to be admired above all others. Now they didn't know what to think at all. They were all shouting and waving their arms in excitement. A few yelled out that they would not be Bábís any more, and then pushed their way out of the tent, never to return.

Meanwhile, Ṭáhirih quietly and calmly walked towards Quddús and sat down beside him. He stood gripping the sword with white-knuckled hands, looking at her as if he would like to kill her. But Ṭáhirih was not afraid. She gazed serenely around the room, waiting until the worst of the shouting had stopped. Then she gracefully stood up and began to speak to the Bábís who were still there. She told them that the old laws and traditions were finished, and that it was time to obey the new laws of the Báb. It was time to let go of the past and go forward to the future. After all, she explained, the veil was just a custom that had grown up in Islámic countries - it was not really a law given by Muḥammad. These old customs and habits had to be left behind now. Slowly the Bábís grew calmer and began to listen to her. 'This is a day to celebrate,' she declared, 'for today the chains of the past have been shattered, and we are free.'

But many of the Bábís remained confused. Quddús and Ṭáhirih still seemed to be angry with each other for a few days. Ṭáhirih said that she thought Quddús was only good enough to be her , and Quddús said that he thought she was leading everyone into making a dreadful mistake. The Bábís took sides; some of them said that Ṭáhirih was right, while others said that Quddús was. They all waited to see what Quddús and Ṭáhirih themselves would do.

At last Bahá'u'lláh quietly came over and sat with the two of them. He talked with Ṭáhirih and Quddús for a long time, while the other Bábís listened.

Quddús and Ṭáhirih travel from Badasht in a howdah

He answered Quddús' questions and explained Ṭáhirih's ideas. When He had finished they were friends again and able to agree with each other. Once Ṭáhirih and Quddús had agreed and become friends, all the Bábís who had taken sides found that they had to do the same.

When the time came to leave Badasht and return to Mázindarán, Quddús and Ṭáhirih discovered that Bahá'u'lláh had ordered a *howdah* for them to travel in together. A *howdah* was like two seats covered with a canopy. It was carried by a mule, and was one of the more comfortable ways for people to travel in those days. Ṭáhirih and Quddús would each have a seat, riding side by side in the *howdah*. Every day of the journey Ṭáhirih wrote a new poem about the dawn of the new age, and all the Bábís travelling with them would chant it with her, until the mountains echoed with their singing.

The Attack at Níyálá

During their journey to Mázindarán, the believers passed through the village of Níyálá.

During their journey to Mázindarán, the believers passed through the village of Níyálá. A few of the Bábís, who did not really understand why Ṭáhirih had taken off her veil, behaved in a shameful way towards the village women. They mistakenly thought that they could now do whatever they wanted.

Mírzá 'Abdu'lláh defending Ṭáhirih from the angry villagers

The Bábís camped for the night near Níyálá and just before daybreak they were suddenly woken up by the crash of falling rocks. The villagers of Níyálá were hurling jagged rocks and stones down at them from the cliffs above. The rocks were smashing into tents and knocking people down as they ran to get away. It was hardly possible to see what was happening in the dim light of dawn. The attackers were shouting 'Bábí! Bábí!' and the wounded were screaming while the hail of stones fell all around them.

Bahá'u'lláh found Quddús lying bewildered and badly hurt, and rescued him from the attacking villagers, who were now pouring down the hillside with axes and clubs raised. He helped Quddús to get away, and told him to go to a safe place and wait there. Then Bahá'u'lláh came back to look for the other Bábís, but found that most of them had been chased away, including the few troublemakers who had upset the women and made the villagers so furious.

The only Bábís still there were Ṭáhirih and a young man called Mírzá 'Abdu'lláh, who was bravely defending her. Even though he had been injured he stood in front of her with his sword at the ready, holding off an angry group of villagers.

Bahá'u'lláh immediately went to help them. Then Mírzá 'Abdu'lláh saw that the gang of villagers had left off trying to seize Ṭáhirih, and had started pawing through all the Bábís' belongings, looking for valuable things to steal. Filled with indignation he rushed at the thieves with his sword, but Bahá'u'lláh called him back before he could fight them again.

Bahá'u'lláh quietly led Ṭáhirih and Mírzá 'Abdu'lláh away from the camp. The villagers stared at them with narrowed eyes, but no one tried to stop them. They were too busy hunting through all the bags and broken tents for loot. Bahá'u'lláh and the other two waited just outside the camp until things had calmed down.

By now the sun had fully risen, and some of the villagers were starting to feel a little bit ashamed. Looking around at the ruined camp in the bright light of day, they saw how far they had gone in seeking their revenge. Bahá'u'lláh gazed at them serenely - even kindly. The villagers felt worse. Seeing that they were now ready to listen, Bahá'u'lláh went and spoke with them as a loving father would speak to his own children.

The villagers listened, glancing doubtfully at each other. They had thought that all the Bábís would be like the few troublemakers among them. Maybe they had been wrong! Finally one of them said, 'I am very sorry for this. I did not know You when I did these things to You and Your friends, but now I do. Here are the things I stole from You. I have decided to give them back.'

When the other villagers saw this many of them also returned what they had stolen, and said that they too were sorry.

Bahá'u'lláh then went to find Quddús, but Quddús was not at the agreed meeting place. Bahá'u'lláh searched for him, and finally, when he could not be found, decided to set off for Mázindarán as they had all planned. In fact, Quddús had been captured, and was being held by his enemies in Mázindarán.

Some people were trying to stir up trouble for Bahá'u'lláh. They had heard of the attack in Níyálá, and thought to themselves, 'At last we have a chance to destroy Bahá'u'lláh!' They went to the King, Muḥammad Sháh, and told him lies about what had happened in Níyálá. They said that all the disturbances there had been Bahá'u'lláh's fault! Eventually they talked the Sháh into believing these lies, and he decided to put Bahá'u'lláh to death.

A message was sent to an officer in Mázindarán. It said that he must arrest Bahá'u'lláh at once, and send Him to Ṭihrán for His execution.

But the young officer who received this message knew Bahá'u'lláh very well, and was His friend. In fact, the message arrived on the very day that this young man was to hold a reception for Bahá'u'lláh at his house. He hid the message away, and tried to think what he could do. Eventually he told the Russian agent at Bandar-Jaz, who went to Bahá'u'lláh and offered him passage on a ship to escape. But Bahá'u'lláh did not run away. He thanked the Russian agent politely, and refused the offer.

That night at the reception the young officer was pale with worry. Bahá'u'lláh saw how anxious he was feeling and smilingly told him, 'Put your trust in God, and you will not be afraid.'

The next day, as He was walking with this same officer, they saw a messenger on horseback tearing down the road toward them. The officer quickly went over to find out what this urgent message could be. When he heard what it was he hurried back to Bahá'u'lláh and gasped, 'Muḥammad Sháh is dead!'

The order for Bahá'u'lláh's execution now meant nothing, for the Sháh who signed it was himself dead. That night the officer ate dinner with Bahá'u'lláh with a peaceful heart. In the morning Bahá'u'lláh left for His home in Núr.

In the meantime the other Bábís who had been chased out of Níyálá were scattering through Persia, telling the believers everywhere about the conference at Badasht, and everything that happened there.

The Visit to Fort Ṭabarsí

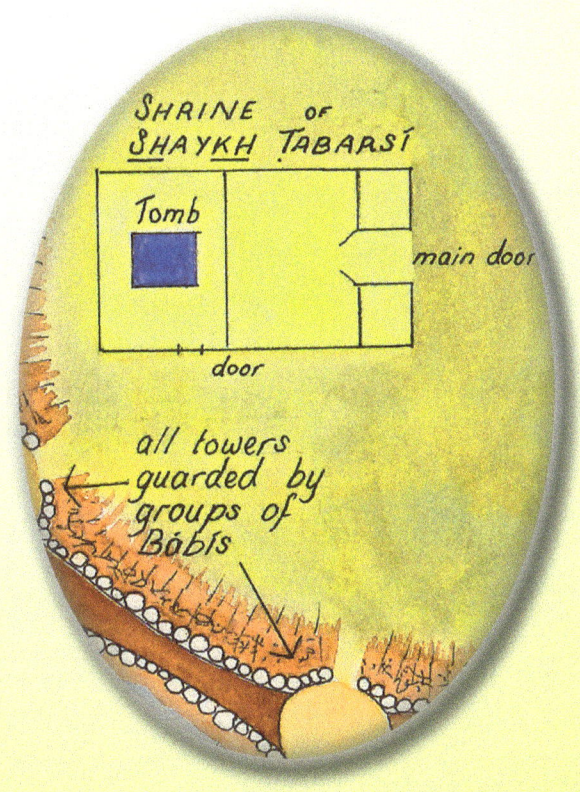

After Bahá'u'lláh arrived back in Núr, he received messages telling Him of what had happened to the other Bábís.

After Bahá'u'lláh arrived back in Núr, he received messages telling Him of what had happened to the other Bábís. Many of them had joined Mullá Ḥusayn, who was travelling to Mázindarán to help Quddús, who was a prisoner there. But on their way they were attacked while resting at the shrine of Shaykh Ṭabarsí. The attack was so fierce that the Bábís had to build a fort around the shrine to protect themselves.

These hastily built walls became known as the Fort of Shaykh Ṭabarsí, where the company of three hundred Bábís sought refuge from the gathering army sent by the Sháh.

When Bahá'u'lláh heard of this He set off for Fort Ṭabarsí to see what He could do to help. When He arrived there Mullá Ḥusayn, who was seeing Him in person for the first time, was so lost in wonder at the sight of His face that he forgot to tell the other Bábís that they could sit down. They were kept standing for a long time until finally Bahá'u'lláh Himself asked them to sit.

Bahá'u'lláh looked over the fort and said that everything had been done well. He told them that if only Quddús was there it would all be perfect. Now this must have seemed like an impossibility to the Bábís. After all, they had been riding to the rescue of Quddús when they were attacked themselves. But Bahá'u'lláh told Mullá Ḥusayn to send seven Bábís to the town of Sárí, to demand the release of Quddús. He assured them that Quddús' captors would be filled with the fear of God when they heard this demand, and would release Quddús without any argument. The seven were sent off without delay.

Then Bahá'u'lláh said that He would return to Núr to get food and medicines and other necessities for the Bábís at the fort. He told them that He would return as soon as He could, bringing all these things with Him.

After He left, the seven Bábís returned with Quddús. Everything had turned out just as Bahá'u'lláh said it would, and Quddús had been released without any trouble at all.

Bahá'u'lláh bought all the supplies needed by the Bábís at Fort Ṭabarsí, and set out to return as He had promised.

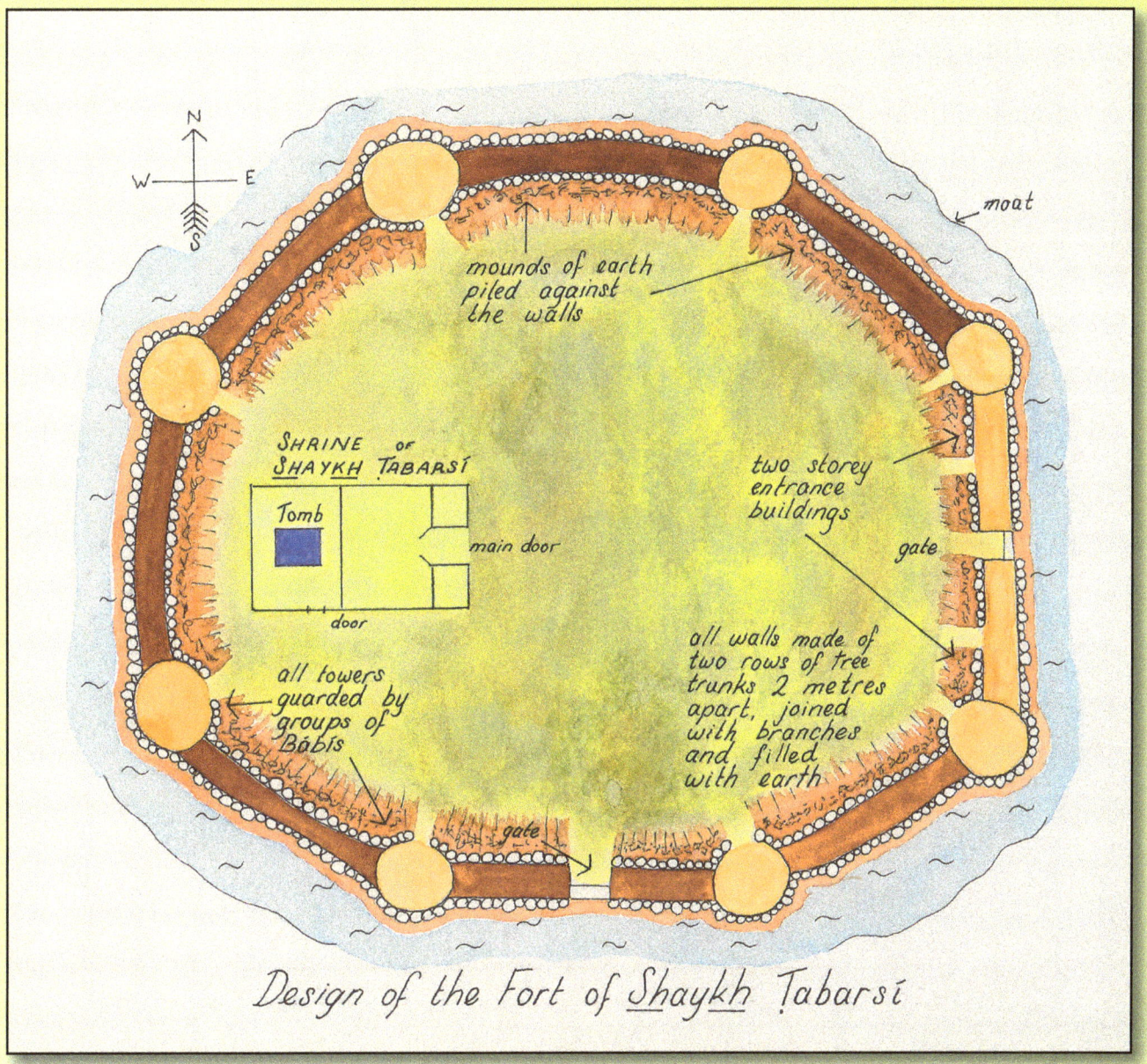

The design of Fort Ṭabarsí

He wished to travel all night without stopping, for He knew there was a risk of being caught if they stopped at all along the way. He brought some of the believers with Him from Ṭihrán, and some of them became very tired during the long journey. They begged Bahá'u'lláh to stop and let them rest. Eventually He allowed them to do so, though He warned them of what might happen.

They stopped at a deserted house about nine miles from the fort, and all the travellers except Bahá'u'lláh lay down to sleep for a few hours. He paced around the house, keeping watch in case of an attack.

Sure enough, spies had seen the travellers arriving at the lonely house, and had gone to inform the officers of the army which surrounded the fort. They sent a troop of riflemen to sneak up on the house.

Bahá'u'lláh saw one rifleman, and then another, and another. The house had been completely surrounded, and there was no way to escape.

The soldiers arrested Bahá'u'lláh and His companions and stole all the supplies which Bahá'u'lláh had brought for the fort. They took the travellers to the town of Ámul. When they arrived the acting Governor of the town recognised Bahá'u'lláh as a nobleman, and insisted that He and His friends should be held in his own house, instead of being put in chains.

This made the mullás (the religious leaders of Islám) very angry. They were determined to stir up as much trouble as they could for the Bábís. They told the acting Governor that he must bring Bahá'u'lláh and His companions to the mosque, to answer questions. Then they told all the townspeople that the Bábís were the enemies of Islám, who must be destroyed.

'Come to the mosque, and bring all your weapons! We are going to question these Bábís!' said the mullás. So the butcher came with his long knives, the carpenter with his axe and the roadmender with his mallet. They waited for the Bábís. The mullás thought that if they could make the crowd angry enough with the Bábís, then the people would all rush at the prisoners and murder them before the acting Governor could do anything to stop them.

When Bahá'u'lláh arrived at the mosque with the other Bábís, the mullás started asking questions. One of them searched the Bábís for any letters, and at last found one. It was a letter written by Siyyid Ḥusayn-i-Kátib. This letter had been written in a great hurry, and was very hard to read.

'Look! Look! a letter in the handwriting of the Báb!' shouted the mullás. Then pointing to a word without studying it carefully one of them added, 'And see, He can't even spell!'

Bahá'u'lláh took the letter from them with gentle firmness, and read out what it said. Siyyid Ḥusayn-i-Kátib had simply written out some words of the

The butcher came with his long knives, the carpenter with his axe, and the roadmender with his mallet

Imám 'Alí. The word which the mullá had said was misspelt was in fact quite a different word, and not spelt wrongly at all. As soon as the mullá realised his embarrassing mistake, he went quiet.

But the other mullás were still trying to make trouble, calling out for all the Bábís to be killed. To prevent this, the acting Governor said, 'I will see to their punishment myself!' He ordered that the companions of Bahá'u'lláh should be bastinadoed. This means that their feet would be whipped on the soles until they were dripping with blood.

Then Bahá'u'lláh intervened. He told the acting Governor that the other Bábís were only His servants and friends, and should not be punished simply for being with Him. He said, 'These are only My companions, and they are blameless. Punish Me in their stead.' This was not what the acting Governor wanted, but there was nothing he could do to stop it now. Bahá'u'lláh was bastinadoed instead of His companions. Then they were all imprisoned in one of the rooms at the mosque.

The acting Governor still feared for Bahá'u'lláh's life, so one night he sent some of his soldiers to break a hole in the clay wall of the mosque and rescue Bahá'u'lláh. He was then brought back to the acting Governor's house. He was still held prisoner, but was safe and well looked after, and His wounds were cared for.

The mullás brought a mob of townspeople to surround the house and demanded to have Bahá'u'lláh handed over to them. The acting Governor went out on the roof and told them that he wouldn't hand over Bahá'u'lláh until he heard from the real Governor, who was fighting the Bábís at Fort Ṭabarsí. He then ordered his guards up onto the roof. They trained their rifles on the mob, and the townspeople scattered back to their homes.

Soon after this the Governor did come back from Fort Ṭabarsí. He was angry when he heard what the mullás had tried to do.
'Why do they pick on these defenceless prisoners?' he asked. 'If they want to fight the Bábís, why don't they go to Ṭabarsí and fight them there?'

The Governor had been so impressed by the heroism of the Bábís at Fort Tabarsí that his feelings about them were quite changed. He was now filled with admiration for them. He went to Bahá'u'lláh and begged His forgiveness for all that had happened. A few days later he arranged for Bahá'u'lláh to be taken back to Ṭihrán, to His own home in that city.

The besieged Bábís at the fort of Shaykh Ṭabarsí fought on bravely for six months and many were killed or died of wounds or hunger. Eight of the Báb's first disciples, the Letters of the Living, lost their lives here, including Mullá Ḥusayn, the first. Bahá'u'lláh had strongly wished to be with the believers at Fort Ṭabarsí, but this wish was not to be granted. Indeed, if He had been able to go there, He would almost certainly have been killed as most of those heroes were. God protected His Messenger in this way, so that He would be able to give His teachings to the world.

Bahá'u'lláh's Letter to the Báb and His Reply

Bahá'u'lláh's house in Ṭihrán became the meeting place for the Bábís who lived there.

Bahá'u'lláh's house in Ṭihrán became the meeting place for the Bábís who lived there. Also, those Bábís who were passing through usually came to stay with Him.

On one occasion, when Vaḥíd, an eminent Bábí, was staying with Bahá'u'lláh, a wild-looking dervish appeared in the doorway. His legs were muddied to the knees, and his clothes were in rags. His name was Sayyáh, and he had just returned from a pilgrimage to Máh-Kú, where the Báb was imprisoned. Vaḥíd knelt and kissed his mud-stained feet, for he had walked on ground that the Báb's feet had touched.

Bahá'u'lláh gave a letter to Sayyáh to take to the Báb. The letter had been dictated to Bahá'u'lláh's half-brother, Mírzá Yaḥyá, and so was in his handwriting. Soon afterward the Báb's reply arrived, praising Bahá'u'lláh and asking Him to see to Mírzá Yaḥyá's education.

Later on that year the Báb, now imprisoned in the remote fortress of Chihríq, began to prepare for His martyrdom. He knew what was going to happen to Him, and was making everything ready. He collected all of His Writings and put them with His pen-case, His seals and agate rings in a locked box. He gave this box to Mullá Báqir, one of the Letters of the Living, and asked him to take the box to Mírzá Aḥmad. He also sent a letter to Mírzá Aḥmad, which contained the key to the locked box. Mullá Báqir delivered the box to Mírzá Aḥmad, who opened it.

Among the things that the box contained was a scroll of fine blue paper. The Báb had written, in His own beautiful handwriting, three hundred and sixty verses in the form of a five-pointed star, and every one of these verses was about 'Bahá'. The Bábís gazed at it in wonder.

Mírzá Aḥmad read the letter from the Báb, and said that he must leave for Ṭihrán immediately. He said that all that he could tell them was that the letter asked him to deliver the box to Bahá'u'lláh. Within the month the Báb was martyred. The Bábís, acting on Bahá'u'lláh's instructions, managed to rescue His body, which had been cast out of the city gates for wild beasts to eat. Bahá'u'lláh arranged for the precious body to be brought to Ṭihrán, where it was carefully hidden.

'Lo, the Nightingale of Paradise singeth upon the twigs of the Tree of Eternity, with holy and sweet melodies ...',

from the Tablet of Aḥmad

The Visit to Karbilá

S oon after the Báb's martyrdom, the <u>Sh</u>áh's chief minister, the Grand Vizier, called Bahá'u'lláh to meet with him.

S oon after the Báb's martyrdom, the Sháh's chief minister, the Grand Vizier, called Bahá'u'lláh to meet with him. This Grand Vizier was the man who had ordered the martyrdom of the Báb, and he was determined to get rid of the Bábís by taking away their leaders, one way or another.

He asked Bahá'u'lláh, 'I think you are now the real leader of the Bábís - is that not so?' Bahá'u'lláh explained to him that this was not true.
'But', the Grand Vizier continued, 'I think that you must be the one who is trying to get people to rebel against our government?'
Bahá'u'lláh told him that the Bábís had not rebelled; they had only tried to defend

Karbilá, the city
Bahá'u'lláh visited

themselves when they were attacked. This was not a plan against the government, it was not organised by anyone.

The Grand Vizier looked at Bahá'u'lláh with hooded eyes. 'Of course,' he agreed smoothly, 'I have no doubt of this. Nevertheless, as the <u>Sh</u>áh is leaving Ṭihrán for a time, I think that it would be better if you were also to leave. Otherwise I might think that you are planning to take advantage of the <u>Sh</u>áh's absence to prepare a plot against him.'
He smiled silkily and added, 'If you do as I ask, I will arrange for you to be given an important position in the government.'

Bahá'u'lláh politely refused the offer of an important position, and told the Grand Vizier that He would be happy to go on pilgrimage to the holy city of Karbilá in 'Iráq. A few days later Bahá'u'lláh left for that city.

At that time a Bábí called Shaykh Ḥasan-i-Zunúzí was living in Karbilá. He had served the Báb as His secretary when He was imprisoned in Máh-Kú and Chihríq. When the Báb heard that both Mullá Ḥusayn and Quddús were trapped in Fort Ṭabarsí, He asked all the Bábís to go there to help them. Shaykh Ḥasan-i-Zunúzí also wanted to go, but the Báb told him not to. He said that Shaykh Ḥasan had something else to do. He said, 'I want you to go to Karbilá, and await the day when with your own eyes you can behold the beauty of the promised Ḥusayn.'

Shaykh Ḥasan had obeyed the Báb, and had been living in Karbilá ever since. One day he was coming out of the Shrine of Imám Ḥusayn after praying there, and found himself face to face with Bahá'u'lláh. Bahá'u'lláh lovingly took his hand, and with a twinkle in His eye said, 'You should thank God that you stayed in Karbilá, for now you have seen with your own eyes the beauty of the promised Ḥusayn.' Shaykh Ḥasan remembered the promise given him by the Báb, and would have shouted out for sheer joy, but Bahá'u'lláh quieted him. It was not yet time for His station to be known.

During His stay in Karbilá, Bahá'u'lláh met as often as He could with the Bábís who were living there. He encouraged them to teach the people of Karbilá more openly, and answered the many questions that they had. After He had been there for some time, the little group of Bábís had become much stronger.

While Bahá'u'lláh was away from Persia, great changes had been taking place. The Sháh had dismissed the Grand Vizier, and put another man in his place. This new Grand Vizier now wrote to Bahá'u'lláh and asked Him to come back to Persia.

The Attempt on the Life of the Sháh

On His way back from Karbilá to Persia Bahá'u'lláh visited a believer named 'Aẓím.

On His way back from Karbilá to Persia Bahá'u'lláh visited a believer named 'Aẓím. He spoke with 'Aẓím sternly, telling him that he must be loyal to the government, and that he must not do anything rash. He warned 'Aẓím that one foolish action might let loose a disaster worse than anything that had gone before. 'Aẓím listened to everything that Bahá'u'lláh said, but did not obey Him. 'Aẓím had a plan hidden in his heart, and he was determined to carry it out.

Bahá'u'lláh continued on His journey, and was staying outside Ṭihrán as a guest of the new Grand Vizier when the disaster struck.

Two young Bábís (who were friends of 'Aẓím) were still half-crazy with grief after the martyrdom of the Báb. They blamed the Sháh for everything that had happened, and wanted their revenge. They waited for the Sháh as he rode out one day. They pretended that they were waiting to ask him for a favour. When he stopped to hear them, they pulled out pistols and shot at him. The pistols were only loaded with birdshot, for these young Bábís really did not know what they were doing. 'Loaded with birdshot' means that instead of proper bullets the guns were loaded with lots of tiny pieces of lead, a soft metal. These are meant to be shot at a flight of small birds, so that the scattering shot sprays into the flock and brings a few birds down. Fired at a person, a gun loaded with birdshot gives that person a fright, and injures him, but certainly could not kill him.

The Sháh's guards pounced on the young Bábís, ripping the pistols out of their hands. Even though they saw how foolish the weapons were, they killed one of the young men on the spot. They questioned the other, asking who had planned the attack. When he would not answer, they poured molten lead down his throat, and so killed him.

As soon as he heard what had happened, Ja'far-Qulí Khán, the brother of the Grand Vizier, sent a message to Bahá'u'lláh, warning Him. At that time Bahá'u'lláh was staying at the home of the Grand Vizier in Afchih. He told Bahá'u'lláh that the Sháh's mother was venomously angry with Him, and was openly telling people that Bahá'u'lláh was the 'would be murderer' of her son. She was also trying to get the Grand Vizier mixed up in the affair, and was saying that he and Bahá'u'lláh had planned the whole thing together. Ja'far-Qulí Khán suggested that Bahá'u'lláh should go and hide with some of His friends until the situation settled down.

Attack on Násiri'd-Dín Sháh by two young Bábís

But Bahá'u'lláh did not hide Himself away. The next day He rode fearlessly out towards the army that was coming to arrest Him.

When He arrived at Zarkandih, a short distance from the army camp, His brother-in-law, Mírzá Majid, came out to meet Him. Mírzá Majid was the secretary of the Russian Ambassador, whose house was in Zarkandih. He invited Bahá'u'lláh to stay at the Russian Legation.

When the officers who were coming to arrest Bahá'u'lláh heard that He had come so boldly to see them they were amazed. They came to the Legation and demanded that the Ambassador hand over his guest, for He was under arrest. But the Ambassador would not give up Bahá'u'lláh. 'I will send Him to the Grand Vizier', he insisted, 'for I do not want Him to be treated unjustly.' And he sent a message to the Grand Vizier saying that if Bahá'u'lláh was harmed he would hold the Grand Vizier to blame, and no one else.

But the Grand Vizier was very frightened by the things the Sháh's mother was saying about him planning the attack with Bahá'u'lláh. He wanted to show that this was not true, so he handed Bahá'u'lláh over to the army.

Now Bahá'u'lláh was dragged out into the road and made to walk through jeering crowds who tore at His clothes and hurled stones at Him. His shoes

The young servant 'Abbás is taken by guards through the streets of Ṭihrán to inform on the Bábís

were snatched from His feet so that He had to walk barefoot on the burning stones of the road. An officer, laughing cruelly, leaned down from his horse and knocked Bahá'u'lláh's hat off, so now the midday sun blazed down on His bare head and neck through all the miles to Ṭihrán.

Trailing behind the crowd was an old woman, too weak to keep up with the mob. She clutched a rock in one twisted hand, and shrieked, 'Give me my chance at Him! I want to throw my rock right in His face!'
Bahá'u'lláh turned to the guard and said, 'Do not disappoint her. She is doing this because she thinks it will please God.' And so He stood still and calm while she struggled up to fling her stone in His face.

Now a pogrom had started in Ṭihrán. Do you know what a pogrom is? That is when members of a particular religion or race, like the Bábís or the Jews, are savagely attacked by everyone else. The police will not help them, and so the mob can do anything it likes to hurt that small group of people. They even see that the government will be pleased with them if they do. This is what happened to the Bábís in Ṭihrán. Filled with horror and hatred by the attack on their Sháh, the townspeople were caught up in a storm of revenge. Anyone who was a Bábí, or was thought to be one, was grabbed from the street and tortured by the mob. Thousands were killed during those days, houses were burned and innocent people burned alive in them. Bábís were beaten to death with hammers, shot from cannons and slashed with knives. Some had burning candles shoved into their wounds, and were made to run down the road with the lighted candles guttering in their flesh.

In the midst of these dreadful events, one of the Bábís, a young servant boy of one of the believers, was forced to betray his fellow Bábís. Under threat of torture, 'Abbás was taken through the streets of Ṭihrán with a gang of guards, and pointed out all the Bábís he saw. Sometimes the guards made him point out rich people who were not Bábís at all. When they cried out, 'I am not a Bábí!' the guards would say, 'Pay us a good bribe, then, or you will be dead before anyone knows the difference.'

Navváb was with her children in their house in Ṭihrán. Suddenly a servant rushed in gasping out the news, 'The Master, the Master, He is arrested - I have seen Him! He has walked many miles! Oh, they have beaten Him! They say He has suffered the torture of the bastinado! His feet are bleeding and there are chains upon His neck!'

Navváb's face grew whiter and whiter, while the children clung to each other and wept. All their servants and friends fled from the house as they heard the news. Only Isfandíyár, their Ethiopian servant, and one black maid bravely stayed. With their help Navváb swiftly gathered together a few clothes for the children and some of her marriage treasures. Clutching these few bundles they hurried away from the house and into hiding.

Soon after that an angry mob boiled through the streets and into the deserted house. The stained-glass windows were smashed, the furniture taken and the treasures looted. Nothing was left.

Navváb was able to move into two rooms quite near the prison. There, she and the children could shelter. When night fell, she took 'Abbás Effendi (who was only eight) and together they crept out to see if they could find out whether Bahá'u'lláh was still alive. Her young daughter, Fátimih, was left behind, cradling her young brother in her frail arms and wondering if her mother and brother would be caught and killed. She sat shivering in the dark of a strange house, waiting and waiting for them to come back.

The Síyáh-Chál

B aháʼuʼlláh had been taken to the Síyáh-Chál, the Black Pit of Ṭihrán.

Bahá'u'lláh had been taken to the Síyáh-Chál, the Black Pit of Ṭihrán. Imagine yourself having walked all those weary miles to Ṭihrán, your feet cut and bloodied by the stony road. Now you are being pushed through a narrow doorway and down steep stone steps. You go down three flights, deep under the ground, and soon every trace of light is gone. You have to feel with your torn feet for the edge of each step, so as not to fall. A choking smell rises up, wrapping around your nose and mouth like a stinking blanket. Suddenly your foot slithers into ankle-deep slime. You have reached the Black Pit.

Bodies shuffle in the darkness, and something squirms in the muck under your foot. Rough hands pull you over to the wall, and push you down, so that you are sitting in that crawling filth. Your feet are locked into heavy wooden stocks, and you hear the clank of a chain being dragged over stone. It is *Salásil*, the most feared chain in Persia. It weighs over fifty kilos. This chain is heaped onto your shoulders and locked around your neck.

That is what happened to Bahá'u'lláh. At first it was not possible for Navváb to get food to Him. For the first few days He had nothing. At last she was able to persuade the jailers to carry a little food down to him, but there was no way of knowing if He had eaten it when there were so many starving prisoners down there.

There were other Bábís with Bahá'u'lláh in the Black Pit, and in the midst of their suffering Bahá'u'lláh taught them to chant this prayer:

'God is sufficient unto me; He verily is the All-Sufficing!' one row would sing, and the other row of prisoners would reply, *'In Him let the trusting trust.'*

Their joyous voices rang out in the darkness, so loudly that the Sháh heard it in his palace. 'What is that noise?' he asked.
'It is the Bábís chanting in their prison', his attendant answered. The Sháh turned his face away and said nothing.

Each day the guards would come and take one of the Bábís to be tortured to death, but none of them was afraid. Bahá'u'lláh had told them that they would be released from this world of darkness and pain, and would fly up in freedom to be with the Báb again. They went out gladly to their deaths, ready to meet their Beloved.

Entrance to the Black Pit, the Síyáh-Chál, the prison where Bahá'u'lláh was confined after the attempt on the life of the Sháh

The Sháh's mother was still determined to have Bahá'u'lláh killed. The servant boy 'Abbás was taken time and again to the prison.
'Identify Him,' whispered the official with him, 'and the Sháh's mother will give you a robe of honour. She will make you her private trustee!'
Then Bahá'u'lláh would be brought into the daylight for him to see.

'Is this the Bábí leader you have told us about?' asked the official. But the boy would look at Bahá'u'lláh (Whom he knew well) and blink dazedly as if he were trying to gaze straight into a bright light. 'I don't know this person,' he would say, shaking his head. 'I don't know Him at all.' And they would have to take him away.

Having failed to get Bahá'u'lláh killed in this way, some of the men of the court decided to please the Sháh's mother by poisoning Bahá'u'lláh. When Navváb brought His food to the prison these men took it and put poison in it. The poison did not kill Him, but it made Him very weak and ill for a long time afterwards.

When the first horror of the pogrom had passed, young 'Abbás Effendi asked to see His Father. The faithful Isfandíyár took Him to the prison and asked the guards to let the little boy see Bahá'u'lláh. They agreed, and took them to the Black Pit. Isfandíyár carried 'Abbás Effendi on his shoulders. They went through a narrow doorway and down the dark stairway. But when they were only half-way down they heard Bahá'u'lláh's voice, saying, 'Do not bring him in here.' So Isfandíyár took Him back up.

They sat outside, waiting for the prisoners to be led out. Bahá'u'lláh appeared in the doorway. He was greatly changed, so ill that He could hardly walk. His hair and beard were tangled and dirty, and His neck swollen and bleeding from the weight of the chain locked around it. He was stooped over, bowed down by the weight of the chain called *Salásil*. 'Abbás Effendi crumpled to the ground in a dead faint at the sight, and was gathered up Isfandíyár's arms and carried home.

During this time of suffering in the Black Pit, Bahá'u'lláh thought deeply about the state of the Bábís. How was it that a group of believers so noble, brave and intelligent could have been capable of making such a foolish attack on the Sháh? He decided that when He left the Black Pit He would devote His life to educating the believers so that they understood the Báb's teachings.

Then, one night He heard a voice surrounding Him in that miserable dungeon. The voice said,
'Verily We will aid Thee to triumph by Thyself and by Thy pen. Grieve not for that which hath befallen Thee, and have no fear.'

From then on, whenever He slept, Bahá'u'lláh felt knowledge and power pouring into Him, like a great waterfall cascading into His Soul. The great Message from God, which would change the whole world, was pouring into Him, and changing Him utterly.

Release from the Síyáh-Chál

Bahá'u'lláh spent four months in the Black Pit.

71

Bahá'u'lláh spent four months in the Black Pit. During that time the attacks on the Bábís continued. Almost all the great heroes and leaders of the Bábí Dispensation had been killed. Quddús had been killed in the public square of his home town of Bárfurúsh, having been taken a prisoner at Fort Ṭabarsí. Mullá Ḥusayn was shot while valiantly defending Fort Ṭabarsí. Vaḥíd, who had led the Bábís during the fighting in Nayríz, had met his death there. The brave Ḥujjat was one of the defenders at the siege of Zanján, dying there with his wife and young child. And Ṭáhirih, who inspired so many, was martyred soon after the attempt on the life of the Sháh.

Only Bahá'u'lláh was left, and He was chained in a dungeon, where He might be sentenced to death at any time. It seemed as if the Faith of the Báb had been completely destroyed. In Qazvín, the Bábís had split into four groups, all fighting amongst themselves. They were without guidance, and growing more and more lost.

The sun of the Báb's teachings had set, and the world seemed to be wrapped in black night. But already the first gleam of a new sunrise had appeared on the horizon, for Bahá'u'lláh was the new Messenger from God, the One promised to the world by the Báb and all the Messengers of the past.

All this time, Bahá'u'lláh's relatives and friends had been trying to help Him. They had prevented Him from being sentenced to death for as long as they could. Now they heard that there was another Bábí, a man called 'Aẓím, in the Black Pit. They were told that he might be the one who really planned the attack on the Sháh. The Russian Ambassador went to the Grand Vizier and told him that he must come to the Síyáh-Chál and question 'Aẓím. Finally the Grand Vizier agreed and sent an official to the Síyáh-Chál with the Ambassador.

When they asked 'Aẓím whether Bahá'u'lláh was the leader of the Bábís who planned the attack on the Sháh, 'Aẓím just laughed. 'The only leader we have is the Báb', he answered. 'When He was martyred I made up my mind to take revenge. I am the one who planned that attack. The young man who threw the Sháh from his horse used to work for me in my shop. He was too hasty, though, and ruined things. It's a pity he didn't wait a little longer, and make certain.'

Both the Ambassador and the official wrote down 'Aẓím's words, and took the confession to the Grand Vizier. Then the Russian Ambassador stood before the court with the written confession in his hand and boldly said, 'Have you not taken enough cruel revenge? Have you not already murdered a large enough number of harmless people? How is it possible that you can even pretend to think that this august prisoner planned that silly attempt to shoot the Sháh?

'You know very well that the stupid gun, used by that poor youth, could not have killed a bird. Moreover, the boy was obviously insane. I have determined to extend the protection of Russia to this innocent nobleman, therefore beware! For if one hair of His head be hurt from this moment, rivers of blood shall flow in your town as a punishment.'

Because of 'Azím's honest and open confession, and also because of the Russian threat, Bahá'u'lláh was set free. Though His enemies still wished for His death, they could not find any reason to inflict the sentence of death upon Him. His innocence was clear. Even so, as soon as He was freed from the Black Pit, the government of Persia issued an order of banishment. Within a month, Bahá'u'lláh and His family would have to leave Persia forever.

The Grand Vizier sent his assistant to the prison to deliver the order for Bahá'u'lláh's release. When this man saw what had been done to Bahá'u'lláh, he was greatly shocked. He could not believe that a nobleman of such well-known good character had been treated so shamefully. Seeing the rags that Bahá'u'lláh wore, he swept his own rich cloak from his shoulders, and begged Bahá'u'lláh to wear it. He did not want Bahá'u'lláh to appear in front of the Grand Vizier and his ministers with the signs of His time in prison clear for everyone to see. Bahá'u'lláh would not accept it. He preferred to appear in front of the ministers of the Sháh's court exactly as He was, a prisoner from the Black Pit.

Still dressed in His prison rags, He went straight to the Court. All the ministers and counsellors stared at Him, and the Grand Vizier burst out, 'If You had taken my advice and left the Faith of the Báb, none of this would ever have happened to You!'
Bahá'u'lláh replied, 'If you had listened to My advice your government would not be in so much trouble.'

The Grand Vizier immediately remembered a conversation he had had with Bahá'u'lláh just after the martyrdom of the Báb, when Bahá'u'lláh had warned

him that the flame lit on that day would soon blaze up more fiercely than before.
'Your warning has come true', he admitted. 'What should I do now?'
'Order the governors of the kingdom to stop killing innocent people, to stop looting their property and hurting their children. Tell them to stop persecuting the Bábís, for they will never wipe out this Faith', answered Bahá'u'lláh.

That same day the orders were sent out to all the governors of Persia, telling them to leave the Bábís alone, but sadly those orders did not stop all the killing.

At last Bahá'u'lláh was free. He came into the two rooms where Navváb and the three children were waiting for Him. How happy they were to see Him again, and to know that He was safe! But how they wept over His illness and His injuries.

His feet, torn and bleeding from the long walk barefoot on rough roads, had been left without bandages or medicine in the filth of the Black Pit. If you have ever had an infected finger, you can imagine the pain He felt. Navváb washed and bandaged those poor feet, and nursed Him as best she could. Both she and the children noticed that He had changed somehow. It almost seemed that there was a bright light within Him, shining out and bringing peace to those who were with Him. Even though He was so ill, and physically very weak, He seemed in some way stronger than ever before.

Navváb struggled to get ready for the exile journey. They only had a month to prepare, and it was now the middle of winter. None of them had proper winter clothes, and a month was not nearly long enough for Bahá'u'lláh to regain His health.

Navváb took out most of her remaining marriage treasures and sold them. With that money she was able to buy some food, blankets and other provisions for the journey. Isfandíyár and the black maid helped her as much as they could. Little Mírzá Mihdí, the Purest Branch, was only four, and not very strong. It was feared that he might not live through the difficult journey, so he had to be left behind with Navváb's grandmother. Navváb was miserable leaving her little son, but there was no choice. She would not see him again for seven long years.

The long winter journey to Baghdád

All too soon the day came when the Holy Family must leave Persia forever. They set off, with Mírzá Músá and Mírzá Muḥammad-Qulí, Bahá'u'lláh's faithful brothers, to help them. With hardly any money, or warm clothing, without even enough food, they began the long winter journey over the mountains to Baghdád.

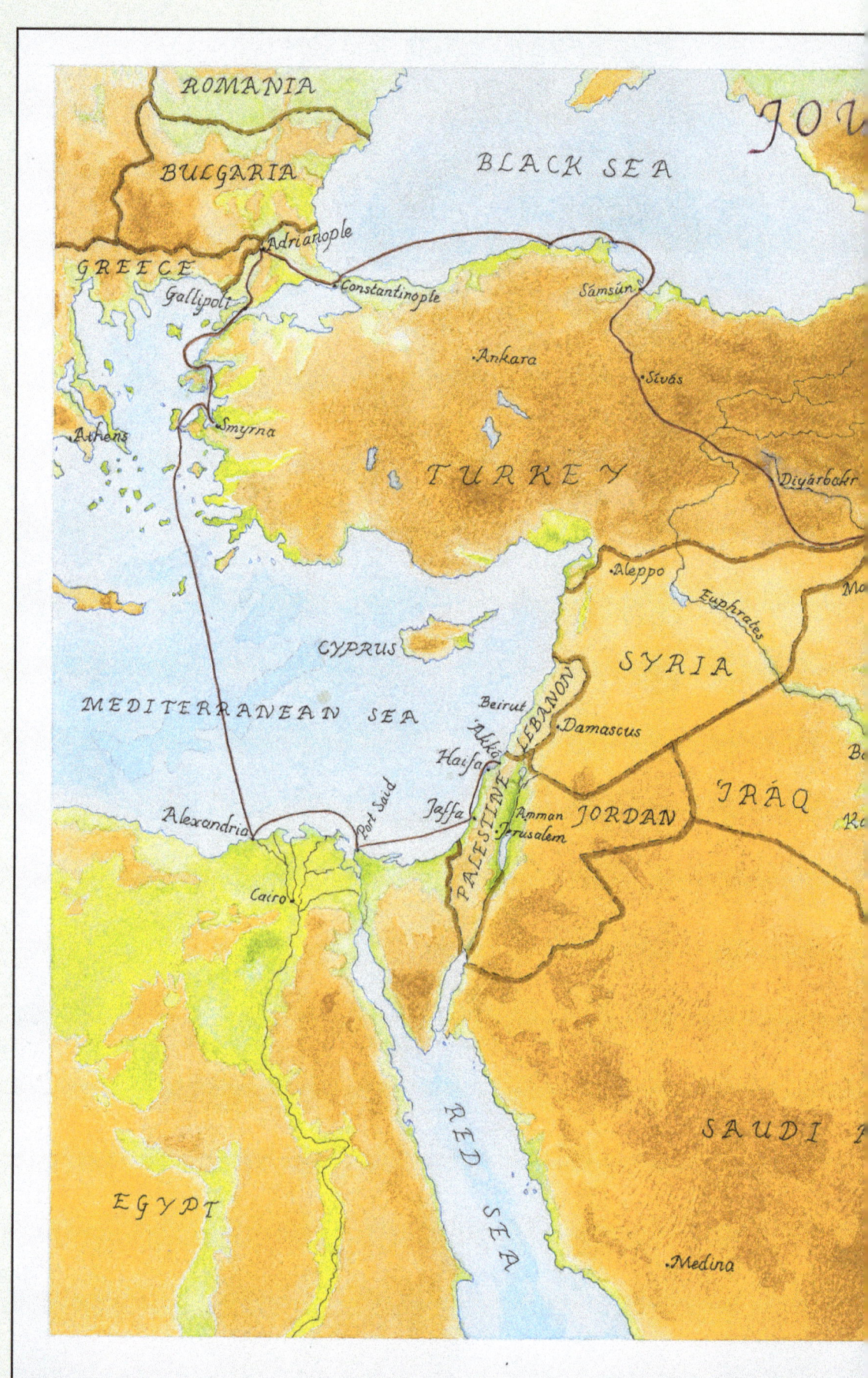

The Journey of Bahá'u'lláh into Exile

The Journey to Baghdád

In midwinter the mountain range between Persia and 'Iráq is covered in deep drifts of snow.

In midwinter the mountain range between Persia and 'Iráq is covered in deep drifts of snow. At times it was so cold that it hurt to breathe, and the travellers could not open their mouths to speak. Sometimes they rode in the travelling litter, slung between two jolting mules, and other times they trudged beside the mules, plunging knee-deep into the snow with every step.

On some nights, they had to camp out in the wild country, huddled together against the cold. When they could, they stayed at a caravanserai. Only one room was allowed for a whole family, and they were only allowed to stay one night at each of these wayside inns, no more. The caravanserais would not allow people staying there to have lamps or candles, so if the exiles arrived after dark, as they usually did, everything had to be managed in the dark. If they were fortunate they might be able to get some hot tea, or a few eggs, but usually they ate only a little hard cheese and some coarse bread. Bahá'u'lláh was still so ill from His time in the Black Pit that He could barely eat the rough food. He was growing weaker still from eating so little.

One day Navváb managed to get a small amount of flour. She put it carefully aside, planning what she might do with it. When they came to a caravanserai, she set out to make a small sweet cake for Bahá'u'lláh. She hoped that He might be able to eat it and so grow stronger again.

She was not allowed to have any light, because of the caravanserai rules, and so worked in the dark. She pulled out the precious package of flour and a small bag of hoarded sugar from her bundle. But in the dark her fingers had found the bag of salt, not sugar. When the cake was brought out it tasted awful. Navváb put her head in her hands and wept. It was almost too much for her to bear, but Bahá'u'lláh gently comforted her.

They were not able to have baths unless they came to a city with public baths. Then, the whole family would go to bathe, and Navváb would take all their clothes and wash them. When she had got them as clean as she could she would carry the cold, heavy bundle of wet things back to their lodgings to dry them - this was almost impossible to do in the freezing damp of winter. Her beautiful slender hands were soon worn rough and red by this work.

Crossing the mountains covered in deep drifts of snow

At last, after three months spent travelling, they reached the Persian border. Bahá'u'lláh sent Mírzá Músá ahead to Khániqayn to rent an orchard. Khániqayn was a town on the border, a few days' journey from Baghdád, in 'Iráq. Spring had come with the end of the journey. Water was babbling in the streams and birds were singing when the Holy Family arrived. Here they were able to stop and rest, breathing the scent of blossoming orange trees and shaded by swaying palms. Bahá'u'lláh told them that everything His enemies had planned to befall Him on the journey had come to nothing.

They had arrived safely.

Party arriving at a caravanserai at dusk

Orange blossoms in springtime

Baghdád

About a month after the Holy Family had settled into a house in Baghdád, there came a knock at the door.

About a month after the Holy Family had settled into a house in Baghdád, there came a knock at the door. Mírzá Músá went to answer it, and found a ragged dervish standing on the step, with begging box in hand. Dervishes were holy men who had no possessions and who travelled about relying on other people's charity.
'Can I help you?' asked Mírzá Músá politely, looking at the dervish doubtfully.
'It's me!' whispered the dervish. 'It's me, Mírzá Yaḥyá! Quick, quick, let me in before someone sees!'

Ever since the attempt to murder the Sháh, Mírzá Yaḥyá, who was Bahá'u'lláh's half-brother, had been in hiding, wandering around Mázindarán disguised as a dervish. But he had begun to think that on the whole it might be safer to get out of Persia altogether, and so had decided to come to Baghdád.

Mírzá Yaḥyá had been trying to convince the believers that he was the real head of the Bábí Faith. He said that the Báb had told him that he was to be the leader of the Bábís. But the Báb had only nominated him as a figure-head, to

86

'People always listen to gossip', said Siyyid Muḥammad

tide things over until the Promised One came. This had not put Mírzá Yaḥyá in danger because he had hidden himself away.

It was the wisdom of God that let Mírzá Yaḥyá go on pretending to lead. This protected Bahá'u'lláh. As long as the Persian Government thought Mírzá Yaḥyá was the leader, they didn't try so hard to harm Bahá'u'lláh. Most of the Bábís understood that Mírzá Yaḥyá was just supposed to be their leader during the time of waiting for the new Messenger the Báb had promised them.

Mírzá Yaḥyá had only been in Baghdád for a short time when he began to notice that something had changed about Bahá'u'lláh. The Bábís in Baghdád almost seemed to be worshipping Him, while they paid no attention at all to Yaḥyá. He began to feel very angry about this. He spoke of it to his friend, Siyyid Muḥammad, who was also feeling very jealous of Bahá'u'lláh. Then Siyyid Muḥammad began to put ideas into Mírzá Yaḥyá's head, about how the two of them together could spread lies about Bahá'u'lláh, and tell the Bábís all sorts of bad and untruthful stories about Him. 'People always listen to gossip', said Siyyid Muḥammad, smiling craftily. 'And the more they listen, the more their hearts will be confused, and they will turn away from Bahá'u'lláh.'

So they went around saying that Bahá'u'lláh wanted power for Himself, and that He was deliberately stopping Mírzá Yaḥyá from doing his job as the head of the Faith. And they told the Bábís all sorts of peculiar things and said that these were the teachings of the Báb. When Bahá'u'lláh heard the strange things that Mírzá Yaḥyá and Siyyid Muḥammad were saying, He spoke with the Bábís, explaining the true teachings of the Báb so that they would not be led astray. But then Mírzá Yaḥyá went around saying, 'See how He contradicts the head of the Faith! You see, He really is after power for Himself, that is why He contradicts me. None of you should listen to Him!'

Bahá'u'lláh knew that the time had not yet come for Him to tell the Bábís that He was the new Messenger. Now, the more He tried to prepare the believers for His Declaration, the more they were confused by Mírzá Yaḥyá. Besides this, He needed time to meditate and think about God, time to hear what God was saying to Him. This was impossible with all the back-biting and confusion among the believers around Him.

At last Bahá'u'lláh could bear no more. He decided to leave Baghdád completely, and to tell no one where He was going. Mírzá Yaḥyá could then have his chance to be the leader of the Bábís. He would be able to see for himself whether the Bábís would turn to him when Bahá'u'lláh was not there, and the Bábís would see whether he really was able to be a good leader.

Before He left, Bahá'u'lláh asked all the believers to treat Mírzá Yaḥyá well. He told Mírzá Yaḥyá to come and live in His house. He also asked Mírzá Músá, Navváb and His children, 'Abbás Effendi and Fáṭimih, to look after Mírzá Yaḥyá well, and to obey him. So you see, He gave Mírzá Yaḥyá every possible chance to succeed.

Bahá'u'lláh had asked the Bábís to recite the prayer, the *Remover of Difficulties* five hundred or even a thousand times, by day and by night. He said this just before He left Baghdád, and after He was gone the faithful believers did as He asked. Although He had spoken at times of leaving Baghdád, none of the believers understood what He meant until He was gone, telling no one where He was going, or even when He might return.

Bahá'u'lláh's Life in the Wilderness

Bahá'u'lláh dressed as a humble dervish, and walked away from Baghdád, far into the mountains of Kurdistán, to Sulaymáníyyih, where He wandered alone, living the life of a hermit.

Baháʼuʼlláh dressed as a humble dervish, and walked away from Baghdád, far into the mountains of Kurdistán, to Sulaymáníyyih, where He wandered alone, living the life of a hermit. He slept in caves, and lived off bread and rice that He had brought with Him. Sometimes, if He had a little milk, He would cook a sort of rice pudding, but this was a rare treat.

When His supplies ran low, He would walk for three days to get to the nearest village and buy more - only as much as He could carry back into the

A little boy came scuffing up the path and sniffing back his tears

mountains with Him. If He grew tired He would sit down at the side of the path and rest.

One day, as He rested, a little boy came scuffing up the path, scrubbing his face with the heel of his palm and sniffing back tears. He saw the Dervish sitting on a rock, and paused, rubbing his toes in the dust and looking doubtfully at the quiet Figure. Was this a truly holy man, or one of those dangerous people who sometimes disguised themselves as dervishes? His father had warned him about them. He decided to walk by on the other side of the path. Just then the Dervish looked up, straight into his eyes, and smiled. His face seemed to shine with beauty, and His smile was so sweet that the little boy simply lost his heart. Without thinking he walked straight to the Dervish and sat at His feet, gazing wide-eyed into that smile. Another sob shook in his chest, but he didn't notice it.

'Little man', said the Dervish gently, 'Why are you weeping?'
Now the tears came fast again. 'Oh sir!' he struggled to speak without choking on sobs. 'The teacher has punished me because I am so stupid and I cannot write properly. But I cannot do it, and I have lost the letters I was supposed to copy from! I am too frightened to go back to school!' He looked up into the Dervish's kind eyes, and saw that He understood it all.
'Do not weep any more', He said. 'I will write the letters out for you to copy, and show you how to imitate them.'

And so He taught the little boy to write there by the roadside. When the lesson was finished, He gave the boy the page of letters in His handwriting, and said, 'Now you can keep this - take it, and show it to your teacher.'

When the teacher saw the page of letters in Bahá'u'lláh's handwriting, he was amazed. 'Who wrote this for you?' he asked, glancing sharply at the boy.
'He wrote it for me - the dervish, on the mountain.'
The teacher tapped his teeth with a fingernail and shook his head slowly. 'That was no dervish who wrote this, but a Prince!' he said. 'No one but a Prince would know how to write this script.'

So the word got out - that there was a wise Prince living somewhere in the mountains, disguised as a dervish. People walked for days, seeking Him out. They brought Him their troubles and questions, which He solved for them; and then those people told others of the wonderful Prince in the mountains, Who knew everything. Bahá'u'lláh had to move further away, to find some peace for meditation.

One evening the Súfís of that area of Kurdistán were gathered together in a village. They were all talking eagerly together about a mystical poem, and wondering about its true meaning, when suddenly a Dervish stood up among them and began to explain it. He brought out deep meanings that were hidden in the poem, so that many of them felt that they had never even begun to understand it before. In that whole listening group of men no one coughed, no one moved. They scarcely breathed as they leaned forward to drink in every astonishing word.

When He finished, they all clustered around Him, eager to hear more. But it was not yet time. One of them asked sadly, 'Oh, Master! Shall we not see You any more?'
He answered, 'In a time to come, but not yet, go to Baghdád and ask for the house of Mírzá Músá of Írán. You will find Me there.' And then He left, walking back into the wilderness.

Without Bahá'u'lláh, the Bábís were soon in a desperate state. Bábís would travel all the way from Persia, in order to see the head of the Faith and ask for guidance. But when they arrived in Baghdád, Mírzá Yaḥyá was nowhere to be found. He was hiding away, refusing to see anyone for fear of being arrested and imprisoned as the leader of the Bábís. When the believers wrote to him with their questions, his replies were so foolish that the questioners felt more muddled than ever. One of the Bábís who received a silly answer to his letter was Dayyán. He began to think seriously about Mírzá Yaḥyá. He carefully studied the Writings of the Báb, and decided that Mírzá Yaḥyá could not possibly be the real head of the Faith. He wrote a long letter to some of the other Bábís, explaining why he thought this. When Mírzá Yaḥyá heard about that letter, he sent one of his servants to murder Dayyán, and also the other Bábís who had listened to him.

In the meantime, Siyyid Muḥammad was in Karbilá, encouraging those who were with him to steal from Muslim pilgrims and even to rob the shrine of the Imám Ḥusayn. The Bábís who truly understood the teachings of the Báb were in despair as they saw what was happening to their beautiful Faith.

One of these people was 'Abbás Effendi, Bahá'u'lláh's eldest Son, whom we know as 'Abdu'l-Bahá. He spent the two years while Bahá'u'lláh was away studying the Writings of the Báb and thinking about the things His Father had taught Him. Though He was only twelve, He saw clearly that without His Father to guide and teach the Bábís, the religion of the Báb would be completely destroyed. He longed with all His heart to see His beloved Father again. Finally one night, He stayed awake through all the dark, silent hours, saying the prayer the '*Remover of Difficulties*' over and over, begging God to let His Father come back.

The very next day, 'Abbás Effendi and Mírzá Músá were walking through the market place when they heard two men talking about a marvellous Person, a wise Prince, Who was living as a Dervish in the mountains of Kurdistán. They listened in amazement and delight. It must be Him! It could not be anyone else!

Two trustworthy believers were sent straight away to Kurdistán to search for Him. Now all the Holy Family could do was wait and hope. Navváb brought out some pieces of precious red cloth, which she had saved from her marriage treasures. Now she would make it into a fine coat, a gift to welcome her Lord. As they waited, the Holy Family's hope grew stronger and stronger. They felt sure that He would be coming home, perhaps even that very day.

Then they heard a familiar step outside - the door opened and He was there. 'Abbás Effendi flew to His side and was wrapped in the rough robes of the Dervish, His face buried in the folds, clinging to His Father's hand as if He could never bear to let it go again.

Life in Baghdád

Once Bahá'u'lláh was back the Bábí community blossomed.

Once Bahá'u'lláh was back the Bábí community blossomed. Hardly any of the believers listened to Mírzá Yaḥyá any more, for now they knew what he was really like. As soon as He was back Bahá'u'lláh called the Bábís together and told them that they must not use violence against anyone. He told them that whatever happened to them because they were Bábís, they must bear for the sake of God. The time for taking up arms against their enemies was past. And He told them that they must obey the laws of the land where they were living.

A few of the Bábís in Baghdád had opened shops. After listening to what Bahá'u'lláh said, they made great efforts to live up to the high standard He had set for them. They began to be known for their honesty and helpfulness, so the shops did very well. Bahá'u'lláh's brothers and sisters in Persia had been able to save some of His property, and now money from these properties was being sent to Him. Soon the poor of Baghdád began to call Him 'Our Father of Compassion', turning to Him for help with all their troubles.

There was one very old lady who lived in the ruin of a deserted house. She knew when Bahá'u'lláh would walk by each day on His way to the coffee house where He taught the Faith. Every day she stood by the road-side, patiently waiting. And every day Bahá'u'lláh would stop and ask if she was well and whether she wanted anything. Then He would put a few coins in her hand. Often she tried to kiss His hand as a sign of her great respect for Him, but He would not allow that. He would bend down so that she could reach His cheek instead. He used to say, 'She knows that I love her, that is why she loves Me.'

Often Bahá'u'lláh would be seen on the banks of the river Tigris, wrapped in His red robe. As He paced up and down beside the swirling water, He revealed the *Hidden Words*, the verses flowing from His lips as swiftly as the river. Sometimes His secretary, writing the words down as Bahá'u'lláh spoke, could hardly keep up.

During His years in Baghdád, Bahá'u'lláh revealed some of the most important and well-known of His Writings, including the *Book of Certitude (Kitáb-i-Íqán)* and the *Seven Valleys*.

Each day in the coffee house, He spoke to the people of Baghdád, telling them of the Most Great Peace that was to come, and of how one day the world would be as one country.

It was not only the poor who came to love and respect Bahá'u'lláh. Clergymen came to sit at His feet and learn from Him. One of them, Áqá Siyyid Mujtahid, said to his friends after meeting Bahá'u'lláh, 'I had been told that the Bábís were wine-bibbers, and that they had no moral principles whatsoever! But when I went to see for myself, I found Purity within Purity. I was amazed to find the exact opposite of that which I had heard. I am absolutely sure that this is the Truth.' And so Áqá Siyyid Mujtahid became a believer.

Even the Governor of Baghdád had become a friend of Bahá'u'lláh. Once, during their last year in the city, 'Abbás Effendi and Mírzá Músá were sent by Bahá'u'lláh to visit the Governor. He gave them such a wonderful welcome that his deputy later said that no one, neither government officials nor important clergymen, had ever been given such a warm and courteous greeting by that Governor.

Even Persian nobles visiting Baghdád were coming to see Bahá'u'lláh to pay their respects and hear what He had to say. One of the princes who came to visit Him decided that he would build an exact copy of Bahá'u'lláh's room in his own palace back in Persia. He thought that if he could copy that room and sit in it he would be able to feel as happy as he felt when he was with Bahá'u'lláh!

When Bahá'u'lláh heard of the prince's plan, He smilingly remarked, 'He may be able to copy this low-roofed room made of mud and straw with its little garden. But can he open onto it the spiritual doors leading to the hidden worlds of God?'

The Persian Consul in Baghdád became very worried by all this. He saw that more and more people were getting to know Bahá'u'lláh, and as soon as they knew Him, they loved Him. He saw that Bahá'u'lláh was going to spread His Faith all through Baghdád, and Baghdád was all too close to Persia's borders. He began trying to get the Governor to send Bahá'u'lláh somewhere far, far away, but the Governor would not listen to him.

So then the Consul wrote to Násiri'd-Dín Sháh, telling him everything that was happening. The Sháh read his letter, and then wrote to the Persian Ambassador in Constantinople telling him to go and talk to the Grand Vizier of the Ottoman Empire. The Persian Ambassador went to the Grand Vizier, and asked him to have Bahá'u'lláh taken out of Baghdád. But the Grand Vizier and

the Sultán had both heard such good things about Bahá'u'lláh that they would not listen either.

Now the Persian Consul was very angry. He hired a fierce bandit called Ridá Turk, and offered him a rich reward if he would murder Bahá'u'lláh. Ridá Turk was delighted to earn such easy money.

He watched Bahá'u'lláh for a few days, and found out when He usually went to the public bath house. Then he waited till he saw Bahá'u'lláh going in, and followed Him. He waited till Bahá'u'lláh's attendant had gone to

Riḍá Turk aimed his pistol at Bahá'u'lláh but trembled and dropped it

fetch something, and sprang out, his pistol levelled at Bahá'u'lláh. Bahá'u'lláh looked up at him calmly. Riḍá Turk found himself gazing helplessly into those compelling eyes, the pistol in his hand completely forgotten. A wave of shame rose over him - and this was a man who had never been ashamed of anything before! He found himself trembling all over, and on the brink of tears. The feeling so frightened him that he turned and fled into the street.

But as soon as he was outside again he began to think once more about the Consul's promise of a rich reward. 'What happened to me in there?' he asked himself angrily. 'I've murdered plenty of other people! How could I let myself be scared off like that?' He smoothed his moustache, frowning to himself as he thought of another plan.

This time he lay in wait for Bahá'u'lláh beside the road He always took on His way back from the coffee house. Now the bandit heard voices, and steps coming down the street. Bahá'u'lláh must be coming!

Riḍá Turk got his pistol ready, thinking, 'This time I'll shoot while He's still far away, so He can't look at me with those sorcerer's eyes.'

He leapt out from his hiding place, and aimed the pistol at Bahá'u'lláh's heart. But again the wave of trembling washed over him. His fingers loosened, and the pistol clattered to the ground. He found himself frozen into stillness, helplessly watching as Bahá'u'lláh and Mírzá Músá walked steadily on towards him.

They stood before Riḍá Turk. With twinkling eyes Bahá'u'lláh turned to Mírzá Músá and said, 'Pick up his pistol and give it to him, and show him the way back to his home. He seems to have lost his way.'

Departure from Baghdád

Bahá'u'lláh was well aware of the Persian Consul's plans to get Him out of Baghdád.

Bahá'u'lláh was well aware of the Persian Consul's plans to get Him out of Baghdád. He knew that the Persian Government might decide to have all the Persian Bábís brought back into Persia, and perhaps put to death. Because of this, He arranged for the Persian believers to get Ottoman nationality, so that they would be protected by the Ottoman Government. The Ottomon Empire was a large portion of the Middle East and was ruled by the Turks. The Persian Consul was very angry when he found out that this had been done.

But the Ambassador in Constantinople kept on and on at the Grand Vizier, because Násiri'd-Dín Sháh was insisting that Bahá'u'lláh had to be taken away from his border. He wanted Bahá'u'lláh to be sent somewhere where He would not meet so many highly placed people. He was really afraid that if Bahá'u'lláh kept on teaching such people, the Bábí Faith would spread back into Persia, stronger than ever before. He thought that sending Bahá'u'lláh further away would stop that from happening.

Now the Ambassador in Constantinople had tried everything, but the Grand Vizier still wouldn't listen to him. At last he was so frustrated that he went into a furious sulk. He locked himself in his house for seven days, and said that he would not be friends with any of the officials he knew any more, and would not speak to any of the Sultán's ministers. Finally the Grand Vizier, who was a very good friend of his, couldn't stand it any more, and gave in. You can see why Bahá'u'lláh later said that He found no one among the government officials of Constantinople who was grown-up enough to understand His teachings. He remarked that they were like children playing with clay.

The order was given for Bahá'u'lláh to leave Baghdád - but instead of being sent somewhere far, far away He was 'invited' to Constantinople itself. This was not what the Persian Ambassador had wanted! Now Bahá'u'lláh would be in the capital city itself, where He could have a great effect.

The Governor of Baghdád gave Bahá'u'lláh a purse of money to use for the expenses of the journey. He did this out of his love for Bahá'u'lláh, so the gift was accepted - and handed out to the poor that same day.

Mírzá Yahyá was still very afraid. He began to think that the invitation to Constantinople might be a trick. Perhaps they were really going to be handed over to the Persian Government after all! What if they were all killed? He decided to leave Baghdád secretly and travel ahead by himself. 'Then if everyone else is killed, at least I shall be safe!' he thought to himself. He didn't even tell Siyyid Muḥammad his plan, but simply disappeared one night. Because of this he didn't travel with Bahá'u'lláh and His companions at first, but met up with them later when he was sure it was safe.

Not all the Bábís were allowed to go with Bahá'u'lláh. Only His family and twenty other believers were to go with Him. The others would have to stay behind and go on with the teaching work in Baghdád. They could hardly bear to lose Him. How would they be able to continue without His wisdom to guide them?

When He came out into the courtyard of His house, the Bábís gathered around Him, weeping aloud. A little boy only three or four years old ran to Him in tears and clung to His robe with both hands begging, 'Oh dearest Master, do not go away and leave us all behind!'

Bahá'u'lláh gently stroked his hair, and told the believers that He must go, in obedience to the invitation of the Grand Vizier of the Ottoman Government. He promised that He would not leave straight away. He was going to a garden just outside Baghdád, and would stay there for twelve days. They would all be able to visit Him there and make a proper farewell.

Not only the Bábís grieved. The streets were crowded with His friends and well-wishers who had come to see Him for the last time. Some threw themselves on the ground at His feet, while others waited to hear a few words from Him. Some just gazed at His face, trying to memorize that last tear-blurred glimpse. The poor were losing their kind Father and the nobles their wise Counsellor. Who would they turn to now, in all their troubles?

Bahá'u'lláh, His sons and His chosen companions were ferried across the river Tigris to the garden. Heavy-laden rose bushes clustered along the paths and tall palm trees swayed overhead. The day was nearly ended and the sun glowed golden behind the latticed trees.

There, in that garden, Bahá'u'lláh made a great announcement. He told those chosen companions the secret He had kept for so long, that He was indeed the Messenger they had been waiting for, the One Whom the Báb had promised

them. Now all their grief at leaving Baghdád melted away as snow melts in spring. Now they understood that Bahá'u'lláh would still be able to give strength to the believers wherever they were, for He was the Manifestation of God. They knew that those left behind in Baghdád would be able to pray to Bahá'u'lláh for help, and that He would always hear them.

Bahá'u'lláh's tent in the Garden of Riḍván

    The days spent in the garden with Bahá'u'lláh were the happiest days the believers had ever known. They named that garden the Riḍván Garden, the Garden of Paradise. Every day Bahá'u'lláh revealed more of His teachings to those who were with Him. The Bábís visiting Him from the city felt strength and knowledge pouring into them as He spoke. Now they knew how they would be able to go on - by obeying His teachings and praying for help.

Only the chosen companions stayed overnight at the garden. Before the dawn of each new day the gardeners would come and pick armfuls of roses from the bushes lining the paths. They would pile these roses in the middle of Bahá'u'lláh's tent in a great mound. Their perfume would fill the room, and when the believers came in to drink their morning tea with Him, they would not be able to see each other over the top of the scented pile. All these roses would be gathered into bunches, and sent to Bahá'u'lláh's sorrowing friends in the city.

Each night some of the companions would stay awake to keep watch by His tent. One night, Nabíl was keeping watch when he saw Bahá'u'lláh leave the tent and walk quietly past the sleeping believers. He paced along the paths, among roses frosted silver with moonlight. Palm trees sighed overhead and the river murmured in the dark. The song of nightingales bubbled out into the night, rising clear and sweet on every side.

Bahá'u'lláh saw Nabíl, and paused a moment to remark that the nightingales stayed awake all night out of pure love for the roses - yet His companions chose to sleep.

Nabíl stayed awake for three nights in a row after that, watching and circling around Bahá'u'lláh's tent. Every time he passed by Bahá'u'lláh's couch he saw that He was still awake. Yet each morning at sunrise He would appear, refreshed and alert, ready to spend the whole day speaking with the stream of visitors flowing in from Baghdád.

All too soon the twelfth day came, and it was time to leave. The mules were loaded and the ladies settled with their children in the *howdah*s. 'Abbás Effendi, who was now eighteen years old, helped the believers make ready for departure. It was nearly sunset when Bahá'u'lláh mounted a red roan stallion and trotted out through the gate. The crowd who had come to see Him off saw that He was indeed leaving, and cried out as one in their dismay.

One of the believers, a man called Mírzá Asadu'lláh, ran after the caravan for three hours, although Bahá'u'lláh had forbidden the Bábís of Baghdád to follow them. At last Bahá'u'lláh saw him panting along behind and got down from His horse to wait for him. He looked lovingly at the heartbroken man and took his hand saying, 'Do not be overcome with sorrow - I am leaving friends I love in Baghdád. You can be sure that I will send news to you all of how we are. Be steadfast in your service to God, and live in such peace as will be permitted to you.'

Then He mounted His horse once again, and Mírzá Asadu'lláh stood watching, his chest heaving with sobs and the fight for breath. Bahá'u'lláh rode steadily off into the darkness. His enemies were powerful and cruel, and no one knew what might happen to Him next.

Mírzá Asadu'lláh catching a last glimpse of Bahá'u'lláh

Constantinople

The spires and domes of Constantinople glistened in the sunlight as the ship steamed into harbour with the company of believers on board.

The spires and domes of Constantinople glistened in the sunlight as the ship steamed into harbour with the company of believers on board. When they came ashore they found that at first they would all be staying in the house of Shamsí Big. Shamsí Big was determined to be a good host, although his house was really too small for so many people. He hired two cooks to help with the work, and the believers did their share too.

Highly placed men came to see Bahá'u'lláh, expecting that He would eagerly ask for their help and support against the Persian Government. Surely He would go to Court and ask for favours from the Sultán and his ministers?

But Bahá'u'lláh said, 'I have no wish to ask for favours from them. I have come here at the Sultán's command. Whatever other commands he gives, I am ready to obey. My work is not of their world; it is of another kingdom, far removed from this world. Why should I seek these people?'

One of the Persian officials was very impressed by Bahá'u'lláh's dignity and His refusal to chase after important people. He said, 'I often feel so ashamed of my fellow Persians, when I see them begging for every possible gift or advantage at Court. It was refreshing to find one Persian who would not do such things.'

After about a month it was possible for Bahá'u'lláh and His family to be moved into a larger house. This house had an area for holding meetings so Bahá'u'lláh could more easily receive all those who wanted to see Him.

Again the Persian Ambassador had to watch His influence grow, as more and more people came to see Him and hear of His teachings. On one occasion a government minister called Kamál Páshá was among the visitors. This man proudly told Bahá'u'lláh how many different languages he had learned to speak. Bahá'u'lláh looked at him sadly and commented that he had wasted his life. He told Kamál Páshá that he and the other officials of the Ottoman Government should choose one language to be a universal language. Then it could be taught to children all over the Empire and later all over the world. In this way, each person would only have to learn two languages - their own, and the universal language. Then people everywhere would be able to talk to each other freely and the world would become as one country.

Kamál Páshá seemed to agree with Bahá'u'lláh and even seemed very happy to hear such a good idea, but he went away and did nothing about it.

The Persian Ambassador watched the stream of high officials and clergymen going to see Bahá'u'lláh, and began to feel worried. How much influence He would gain if He stayed in the Empire's capital! In Baghdád, the longer He stayed the more people grew to love Him - what if that happened in Constantinople? It would be far worse! He received message after message from the Sháh, telling him to get Bahá'u'lláh away from Constantinople and to stop Him from gaining so much influence.

So the Persian Ambassador began spreading lies about Bahá'u'lláh. When Bahá'u'lláh did not go and beg for gifts and money at Court, this Ambassador said He was too proud to see anyone, and that was why He did not come. 'He has no respect for the Sultán - He will have no respect for your laws, any more than He respected our law in Persia', whispered the Ambassador. 'Soon He will start a rebellion against your government - you wait and see!' And the foolish Court officials, who could not even begin to understand Bahá'u'lláh's spiritual purpose, believed him.

No matter how many times Bahá'u'lláh explained to these people that He did not care about the things of this world, they did not understand Him. They kept thinking that He must want power and wealth, just as they did. Now they began to think that He really might be planning a rebellion. And they thought to themselves that people loved Him so much, He would be able to call thousands of them to follow Him. He would indeed call thousands, and then millions, but He would call them to obedience, not rebellion.

Only four short months after Bahá'u'lláh's arrival in Constantinople, He was banished to Adrianople, at the furthest end of the Empire. Again, the journey would have to be made in the dead of winter.

On the same day that the Sultán's order of banishment arrived, Bahá'u'lláh sent him a Tablet of Proclamation. In this Tablet He called on the Sultán to believe in Him, and promised that he would face the justice of God if he turned away from His Messenger.

    The Tablet was sealed in an envelope and given to S̲h̲amsí Big to deliver to the Grand Vizier. Bahá'u'lláh told S̲h̲amsí Big to say that the Tablet was sent down by God. It was not meant as an answer to the Sultán's order of banishment.

    S̲h̲amsí gave the envelope to the Grand Vizier, who ripped it open with a snort and began to read. As he read it his face turned greenish-white with

112

The Grand Vizier's face turned greenish-white with shock

shock, as he gasped, 'He sounds like the King of Kings giving orders to one of the least important little kings in His Empire! Why, He is taking it upon Himself to correct the Sultán's behaviour!'

The Grand Vizier looked so upset that <u>Sh</u>amsí Big hastily backed out of the room, and went back to tell Mírzá Músá what had happened.

Bahá'u'lláh later told the believers that the Sultán might have had some excuse for the things he did after reading that Tablet. But for the things he did to Bahá'u'lláh before reading it, he had no excuse at all.

Just before leaving Constantinople, Bahá'u'lláh sent a message to the Persian Ambassador. He told the Ambassador that it had been no use at all killing and torturing so many Bábís. He said that now there were a hundred times more Bábís than before, and that none of his plans to get rid of them would ever work, for this was the Cause of God.

Now the company of believers set off once more, to another strange land. Once again there was no time to prepare, and none of them had warm enough clothes. The women and children had to pile into goods carts, for there was no other transport available. This journey took place during the worst winter anyone could remember for more than ninety years. Even the Euphrates river, which they had crossed on their journey from Baghdád to Constantinople, froze over completely, which was unheard of. When the believers needed water on their journey they had to light a bonfire near a frozen stream and wait for the ice to melt. Travelling through sleet and storms, sometimes even walking through the night with their escort of Turkish soldiers, the exhausted exiles at last arrived in Adrianople.

Adrianople

The people of Adrianople soon grew to love and respect Bahá'u'lláh.

The people of Adrianople soon grew to love and respect Bahá'u'lláh. It was always the same story. Those who came to see for themselves loved Him, and those who listened to backbiting never found out what He was really like. The Governor of Adrianople and many other officials came to see Him and to ask Him their questions. Word spread around the city. People spoke of His wisdom, and of His kindness. Sometimes, when He walked through the market place, people would stand up and bow to Him, for they saw that He was a great and holy Man.

Now Bahá'u'lláh told the believers that they should go out and get jobs. He said that they should do this so that they would not be bored, and could earn money for themselves. So every day the believers went out to their jobs and every night they came to Bahá'u'lláh's house to eat, read prayers and hear Bahá'u'lláh speak.

But Mírzá Yahyá's anger and jealousy were growing stronger every day. The more he saw how Bahá'u'lláh effortlessly attracted the hearts of those around Him, the angrier he got. To make matters worse for Yahyá, even Siyyid Muhammad had begun treating him like a fool. Once, when Yahyá tried to answer a question from a believer, Siyyid Muhammad laughed aloud in scorn at his silly answer, and told everyone that it was quite wrong. Yet this same Siyyid Muhammad was busily writing letters to the believers in Persia, telling them what a great man Mírzá Yahyá was. You can see that what Siyyid Muhammad wanted was a leader of the Faith whom he could easily control. With Mírzá Yahyá as leader, Siyyid Muhammad knew that he would be able to do exactly as he pleased.

One of the believers in Persia wrote back to Siyyid Muhammad, and asked, 'If Mírzá Yahyá is so wonderful, why is it that he won't answer our questions? And how is it that Bahá'u'lláh writes such amazing books as the *Kitáb-i-Íqán* if He is the bad person you say He is?' Siyyid Muhammad quickly wrote back and said, 'You see, Bahá'u'lláh has Yahyá chained in a cellar, and whips him till poor Yahyá has to tell Him how to answer your questions.'

Of course no one sensible could take a foolish story like that seriously. Even the believers who had never met either Bahá'u'lláh or Yahyá were able to see Who was the true Leader of the Faith.

Aḥmad on his travels to find the Promised One

Now Bahá'u'lláh decided that the time had come to tell all the believers that He was the new Manifestation. The Declaration in the Garden of Riḍván had only been made to His family and trusted companions. The believers in Persia, Syria and 'Iráq still thought of themselves as Bábís. Bahá'u'lláh sent Tablets with faithful messengers who travelled everywhere to give the news.

One of those who taught the new Faith of Bahá'u'lláh to the Bábís all through Persia was a man called Aḥmad. Aḥmad was the son of a rich and powerful family from Yazd. But Aḥmad did not wish to follow in his father's footsteps. Even in his early teens, Aḥmad was spending much of his time praying and fasting, for he was filled with a longing to see the Promised One. Somehow he felt sure that the Promised One was on earth, and he wished with all his heart to be able to find Him. Aḥmad's family were not pleased with his behaviour, and did their best to push him toward a more practical approach to life.

Eventually, Aḥmad decided that he would have to leave home if he was to find the Promised One. He set off one morning with a small bundle of clothes, saying that he was going to the public baths. But instead, he left the city and began his long search. He roamed through Persia, dressed as a beggar, going from holy man to holy man, asking each one how he could find the Promised

One. He travelled on to India, always asking the same question. Once, he was told that if he said, 'There is no God but God' twelve thousand times over, then he would find the Promised One. On several occasions Aḥmad knelt and repeated those words twelve thousand times, but still he did not find the One he sought.

At last Aḥmad went back to Persia, disappointed and saddened by the failure of his search. He didn't go back to Yazd, but stayed in the city of Káshán, where he married and set up shop as a weaver. But in his heart, Aḥmad was still searching.

After a while, rumours about the Báb and His followers reached Káshán. Aḥmad became very interested by what he heard, and began asking questions about the Bábí Faith, trying to find out more about it. One day he met a traveller at a caravanserai, who told him to go and ask a certain mullá in Mashhad if he wished to know the truth.

The next morning, Aḥmad set off for Mashhad, walking all the way. After a few days there, Aḥmad had learned enough. He knew that he had found the truth at last, and became a Bábí. He went back to Káshán, and soon found that there was one other Bábí in that city, a man called Hájí Mírzá Jání.

One day Hájí Mírzá Jání came to Aḥmad and told him that the Báb was to be brought through Káshán as a prisoner. He had been able to persuade the authorities (who did not know he was a Bábí) to let the Báb stay for two or three nights at his house.

Aḥmad went to Hájí's house the evening the Báb was there. He saw a young man, who had the most beautiful face he had ever seen. The religious leaders of the city were all there, ready to ask the Báb questions. They wanted to prove that He was a wrongdoer. But the Báb answered all their questions with such courage and grace, Aḥmad, who was sitting unnoticed at the back, thought that anyone with ears to hear and eyes to see should have believed in Him straight away.

When tea was served, the Báb accepted His cup, then called the servant of one of the religious leaders. Smiling sweetly, he gave this man His own tea to drink. The next day that same humble serving man came to Aḥmad, asking if

Aḥmad hid in the wind tower

he knew of anyone who could tell him more about the religion of the Báb. So Aḥmad taught him, and he became a Bábí.

Now there were three Bábís in Káshán, and the number slowly grew larger. As the little community grew, the religious leaders of the city were angered. They preached against the Bábís, and sent mobs to tear down their houses and steal their belongings. When the mob came to find Aḥmad, he hid in a wind tower, and the mob did not find him. This wind tower was like a tall, wide chimney. It wasn't there to let smoke out, though. It was there to catch cool breezes and send them down through the house to cool it. Aḥmad had to stay hidden up there for forty days, with only the small amounts of food and water that his friends were able to bring him secretly at night.

Aḥmad decided that life in Káshán was impossible. When he was able to escape from the wind tower, he left the city, climbing over the walls in the middle of the night. He had heard about Bahá'u'lláh, and decided to go to Baghdád, to visit Him.

When he reached Baghdád, he went straight to the house of Bahá'u'lláh. He was taken inside, to the room where Bahá'u'lláh was speaking with some of the friends. When Aḥmad walked into the room and saw the face of Bahá'u'lláh, he was overcome. He stood gazing in bewilderment and love, and was only brought back to earth by the laughing voice of Bahá'u'lláh teasingly saying, 'What a man! He becomes a Bábí and then goes and hides in the wind tower!'

Aḥmad was allowed to stay in Baghdád, living in a room behind Bahá'u'lláh's house. He worked as a weaver, and in the evenings listened to everything Bahá'u'lláh said, learning all that he could during those six wonderful years. Then the Sultán's 'invitation' to Constantinople came, and Bahá'u'lláh had to leave Baghdád. Aḥmad was one of those left behind to teach the Faith in Baghdád.

He tried very hard to teach, and to be happy staying in Baghdád, but the longing to see Bahá'u'lláh again grew and grew in his heart.

He heard that Bahá'u'lláh was now in Adrianople, and at last decided to follow Him there. When he stopped at Constantinople on his way to Adrianople, he found a letter from Bahá'u'lláh waiting there for him. He opened it, and found the *'Tablet of Aḥmad'*. If you look in your Bahá'í prayer book you will find this special prayer there.

Aḥmad sat and read his Tablet over and over, filled with the sincere wish to know what Bahá'u'lláh wanted him to do. As he read it, he understood. He already knew that Bahá'u'lláh was the new Manifestation of God. Now he saw that he must go back to Persia and teach the other Bábís about Bahá'u'lláh, so that they would understand who He truly was, and become Bahá'ís. He knew he must give up his own longing to see Bahá'u'lláh, and go back to teach His Faith. Whatever happened, Aḥmad knew that he would always have his precious Tablet to protect and help him, for in it Bahá'u'lláh said,
'By God! Should one who is in affliction or grief read this Tablet with absolute sincerity, God will dispel his sadness, solve his difficulties and remove his afflictions.'

The Poisoning

T he Promised One had revealed Himself at last! As they heard the news, the Bábís rejoiced.

The Promised One had revealed Himself at last! As they heard the news, the Bábís rejoiced. Many of them had already guessed who Bahá'u'lláh was, and the rest had learned so much of His compassion and great knowledge that they were not surprised. Ninety percent of them became Bahá'ís straight away. Some decided to stay as Bábís, and only a very, very few were left who would listen to Siyyid Muḥammad and Yaḥyá.

The two were enraged. And now Yaḥyá began to think of a dreadful plan. He saw that he would never be leader as long as Bahá'u'lláh lived. Even when Bahá'u'lláh went away to Kurdistan, people couldn't stop thinking of Him and longing for Him. No one had a moment's thought for Yaḥyá, except to wish that he was somewhere else. But if Bahá'u'lláh were dead? Then they would turn to the only other person ready to lead, thought Yaḥyá. Then he could take over.

In the meantime, pilgrims had begun to come from Persia, Syria and 'Iráq to see Bahá'u'lláh. He was now revealing tablets and verses so swiftly that 'Abdu'l-Bahá, Mírzá Mihdí (the Purest Branch) and Mírzá Áqá Ján, Bahá'u'lláh's secretary, were all kept busy from dawn till dusk taking them down and making copies.

In the midst of all the happiness and busy work of the new Bahá'í community, Mírzá Yaḥyá laid his wicked plans. He learned how to make poison, and then began to invite Bahá'u'lláh to take tea with him, as if he wanted to be friendly again. Before one of these visits he smeared Bahá'u'lláh's teacup with poison, and when Bahá'u'lláh drank, he thought the evil deed was done.

Bahá'u'lláh lay near death, His body wracked with pain and fever. A Christian doctor called Dr Shíshmán was called in to see Him. The doctor looked at his Patient in dismay. Bahá'u'lláh's face was a leaden grey, and when He wiped His mouth with a handkerchief it came away soaked with blood. Tears came to the doctor's eyes as he knelt beside the bed. 'There is no medicine that will cure this', he said, and then left the room. The Bahá'ís looked at each other in despair.

But Dr Shíshmán went to his home and offered up a heartfelt prayer. He prayed that God might take him instead, and allow Bahá'u'lláh to remain in this world. Although not a Bahá'í, the doctor knew what a great and holy person Bahá'u'lláh was.

Mírzá Yaḥyá smeared Bahá'u'lláh's teacup with poison

That night, Dr Shíshmán fell ill, and Bahá'u'lláh miraculously began to get better. Áqá Ján went to visit the doctor, to see if there was anything he wanted. Dr Shíshmán smiled and weakly shook his head. 'I am content', he said, 'for God has answered my prayer. If you need a doctor, you should call on Dr Chúpán - he is very reliable.' A few days later he died.

Bahá'u'lláh slowly recovered. For the rest of His life His hands would shake as a result of this poisoning. After six long weeks He was able to rise from His bed and walk to a nearby garden to sit in the shade of the trees. He went to this garden each afternoon while He gradually grew stronger, and after work the Bahá'ís gathered there, knowing that they would see Him. One afternoon Bahá'u'lláh asked for news of a believer who was ill, but no one knew how he was. Bahá'u'lláh remarked that He Himself should have gone first to visit the sick man, before coming to the garden. 'This I tell you', He went on, 'that you all should learn to care for one another at all times, and look after each other.'

The poisoning of Bahá'u'lláh had one very important effect. All the Bahá'ís knew who had done it, and from then on the last few simple men among them who were still muddled became absolutely sure in their own hearts about Yaḥyá. They knew now that he was a wicked man, who could not possibly be the proper leader of their Faith. Now the only ones who stayed with Yaḥyá were wicked people like him.

When He was well again Bahá'u'lláh sent a special Tablet to Yaḥyá, clearly and plainly announcing Himself as the new Messenger from God. He did this so that Yaḥyá would not be able to make any more excuses, or pretend that he had misunderstood.

The Tablet was delivered to Yaḥyá, but he refused to answer straight away. He said he needed time to think. The very next day Yaḥyá's answer came - he said that he had a revelation from God, and everyone ought to bow down before him. Now Yaḥyá had really gone too far. In the past he had done terrible things to Bahá'u'lláh and had been forgiven. But now he had offended against God, and Bahá'u'lláh would not allow him to do that.

This was the time that is called the Most Great Separation. Bahá'u'lláh gave Yaḥyá his share of the family's funds and other belongings and sent him away. He and Siyyid Muḥammad and those who wanted to be with them would no longer be allowed among the true believers.

Then Bahá'u'lláh did the same thing He did the last time Yaḥyá was trying to split up the believers. He went away from them all and let the believers freely choose what they would do. This time He only stayed away for two months, and remained in His house so that they all knew where He was. But it was still a very difficult time for the Bahá'ís, who missed Him dreadfully.

When Bahá'u'lláh let them come and see Him again the few wicked men among them had gone to Yaḥyá, never to return. The poison of hate and envy had been cleaned out of the community, and it was made whole again.

The Tablets to the Kings

One day in Adrianople as Bahá'u'lláh was pacing around the courtyard of His house, He remarked to His companions, 'Today We wrote something to Násiri'd-Dín Sháh - but who will bell the cat?'

One day in Adrianople as Bahá'u'lláh was pacing around the courtyard of His house, He remarked to His companions, 'Today We wrote something to Násiri'd-Dín Sháh - but who will bell the cat?'

This is the story He was referring to. Once there was a fierce cat who terrorized all the mice around. Finally, the oldest and wisest of the mice said, 'My friends, if only we could put a bell round the cat's neck, then we would be able to hear him coming.'
'Yes, indeed!' agreed the other mice. 'But who will bell the cat?' And no mouse could be found who was brave enough to do it.

It was very different with the Bahá'ís. Many of them came to Bahá'u'lláh to beg for the honour of delivering that Tablet to the Sháh, though they knew

Badí' and his torturers

it meant certain death. Bahá'u'lláh would only say that He was waiting for someone special. It was not until Bahá'u'lláh was in 'Akká that this special person appeared.

That person was Badí'. He was a boy from a good family, and his father was a Bahá'í, but he was the despair of his parents. He was an angry and unhappy young man, who would not listen to his father, or do anything he was told. But one day Nabíl-i-A'ẓam visited the family of Badí' in the town of Nishápúr, and stayed in their home. That night, Nabíl told Badí' all about Bahá'u'lláh and he became a Bahá'í. In obedience to his father, Badí' then began to learn to read and write and to study Bahá'u'lláh's teachings. Before long, however, his longing to see Bahá'u'lláh was so great he walked all the way to 'Akká, to go on pilgrimage.

When Badí' saw Bahá'u'lláh he seemed to change into a completely different person. He became calm and happy, and was filled with faith. When Bahá'u'lláh asked him to take the Tablet to the Sháh, he agreed with delight. Bahá'u'lláh warned him that he would surely die, but Badí' was not afraid. He went straight to the Sháh, travelling non-stop on foot for four months. When he was brought before the Sháh he cried, 'O King! I have come to thee from Sheba with a weighty message.'

The Sháh immediately knew Who the message was from, and had Badí' arrested. The guards tortured Badí', trying to get him to tell the names of other Bahá'ís so that they could be arrested too, but he said nothing. To their shock and surprise, he laughed even as they pressed burning brands on his skin, and seemed to feel

Emperor Napoleon III throws Bahá'u'lláh's Tablet aside

nothing. When they saw that he could not be broken, they killed him, crushing his head with a hammer. He had only just turned seventeen.

The Tablet to the Sháh clearly explained that Bahá'u'lláh was the Promised One. It said that, as a good Muslim, the Sháh should accept what He said, for His words were from God. But the Sháh paid no attention.

Other Tablets were sent to the kings and rulers of the earth. Some of these were sent from Adrianople, and some from 'Akká. One was sent to Napoleon III, who was then at the height of his success. He contemptuously threw it aside, saying, 'If this man is God, I am two gods.'

Bahá'u'lláh wrote him a second Tablet, now warning him that for what he had done he would lose his entire empire. Within a year this had happened, and Napoleon was utterly defeated. The French agent in 'Akká who had translated and sent the Tablet became a Bahá'í after seeing Bahá'u'lláh's prophecies come true.

Bahá'u'lláh also wrote to the German Emperor, warning him of what would happen if he did not stop building up his supply of weapons and instead start working for peace in the world. Bahá'u'lláh said that if the German Emperor did not do this then German soil would be soaked with blood, not once, but twice. The German Emperor did not listen, and we have seen the two world wars that happened as a result.

He wrote to the Queen of England and praised her for her good work in stamping out the evil practice of slavery in the British Empire. He also said that He was pleased that she had allowed elections to take place in her country, so that some of the power was now in the hands of the people. He told her that the problems of the world would never stop until the kings of the earth united to put an end to war. It is said that the Queen read the Tablet and commented, 'If this is from God, it will endure; if not, it can do no harm.'

Bahá'u'lláh did not send a letter to the rulers of America, but in His *Most Holy Book*, the *Kitáb-i-Aqdas*, He spoke to them, telling them that He was Christ, returned at last. He said that they must defend the weak and help the victims of injustice, for this was the command of God.

There were many other Tablets, to the Sultán, the Pope and other rulers. But none of them tried to find out if He truly was Who He said He was. Because they all turned away from Him, or ignored Him, the chance of stepping quickly into the Most Great Peace without pain or struggle was lost forever. Bahá'u'lláh said that now the people of the earth should do their best and work for the Lesser Peace. He said that this Lesser Peace would eventually grow into the Most Great Peace, after hundreds of years of work and suffering. The rulers of the earth rejected the Promised One, and now the hard road to peace was the only road left for mankind.

Adrianople
The Last Years

T he days in Adrianople flowed by.

The days in Adrianople flowed by. The believers no longer had to worry about Mírzá Yaḥyá in their midst. They rarely saw him, and were able to get on with their daily lives in peace. Pilgrims came to see Bahá'u'lláh, and Tablets continued to be revealed at a rapid pace. Mírzá Áqá Ján wrote so quickly trying to keep up that sometimes the pen flew out of his hand. There was no time to fetch it - he would seize another and go on writing. As each page was filled it fell to the floor and another was begun. By the end of a morning's work, the floor would be littered with sheet after sheet of Revelation. You can see how it came about that the whole of the *Book of Certitude (Kitáb-i-Íqán)* was revealed in only two days.

Yet one day Bahá'u'lláh turned to His companions and remarked, 'This is a fine place and a fine province. But I do not wish that we stay here. Before long all will be changed.' The Sultán may have thought that he was ordering Bahá'u'lláh about from place to place, but the reality was quite different. No one moved Him unless He wished to be moved. From that day on He often spoke of the changes that were coming. He asked some of the believers to leave Adrianople, saying, 'Why should we all be imprisoned, and no one be left to teach the Cause of God?'

He knew quite well what was about to happen. Separated from the Bahá'í community, Yaḥyá and Siyyid Muḥammad made one last effort to challenge Bahá'u'lláh. Yaḥyá wrote to the Governor, complaining about Bahá'u'lláh. He did this to try to make trouble. The Governor knew Bahá'u'lláh well, and he took Yaḥyá's letter to Him, and asked Him what to do. Bahá'u'lláh replied, 'Ask him to come and see Me. If he comes, then whatever he says is right.'

The Governor went to Yaḥyá, and asked him to go and see his Brother. Yaḥyá said, 'We do not go to each other's houses, and He will not come to the Governor's house.' So the Governor suggested that they could meet in the mosque, and Yaḥyá had to agree.

On Friday morning Bahá'u'lláh set off for the mosque. The people of Adrianople had heard that He was to go there, and they crowded the streets between His house and the mosque. The streets were so full of people that the traffic was stopped. They called out to Him, asking for His blessing. He answered over and over, 'Greetings! Greetings! May God bless you all!'

When He walked into the mosque, the preacher on his pulpit stopped his sermon in mid-sentence, standing there silent until Bahá'u'lláh gave him permission to continue. Everyone waited for Yaḥyá to appear and meet with Bahá'u'lláh as he had said he would. They waited for a long time, but Yaḥyá never came. After this, everyone in the city knew that Yaḥyá was not a truthful person, and they did not listen to him any more.

When they found that they could not get anyone in Adrianople to believe their lies about Bahá'u'lláh, Siyyid Muḥammad went to Constantinople to see the Persian Ambassador. They spoke together many times, laying their plans. After that, Siyyid Muḥammad went to the Court of the Sultán, and told the Ottoman officials that the pilgrims visiting Bahá'u'lláh were actually rebels in a conspiracy with the Bulgarians, and were getting ready to attack Constantinople! It seems strange now to think that the Sultán could have believed these lies, but he did. He and his ministers were so frightened that they decided to arrest Bahá'u'lláh, and banish Him yet again.

The whole plot backfired on Yaḥyá in the end. He too was banished, to the lonely island of Cyprus, where he lived out the rest of his days, little remembered and unmissed.

When the Governor of Adrianople received the order banishing Bahá'u'lláh, he refused to carry it out. His deputies had to take over from him and organize the arrest, for the Governor knew and loved Bahá'u'lláh, and would not do anything to harm Him.

Early the next morning, soldiers surrounded Bahá'u'lláh's house, and would not let anyone in or out. The foreign consuls in Adrianople heard of what was happening, and came in a group to see Bahá'u'lláh and ask if there was anything they could do. Bahá'u'lláh gently refused their offers to force the Ottoman Government to change its mind.

The consuls still visited Him, and the soldiers guarding the house could not stop them because of their status as diplomats. The major of the brigade threatened to punish his soldiers if they let the consuls through one more time, but it was no use. They were foreign officials, and could not be stopped. 'Abdu'l-Bahá told the consuls about the brigade major's blustering threats, and

Mosque of Sultán Salím in Adrianople, the meeting place set for Bahá'u'lláh and Mírzá Yaḥyá

they were much amused. One of them joked that they had better be sure to send the British Consul through first next time, so that he would be the one to take a beating from the brigade major!

Most of the Bahá'ís' belongings were taken away and sold for less than half their worth. They were then given the money from that forced sale - or most of it. They had to pack what was left and get ready to leave. The people of Adrianople came to the house, but the soldiers would not let them in to say their goodbyes. They stood in the street and wept, the Christians more than anyone.

The Bahá'ís were brought out. Their luggage was loaded into wagons and they climbed in after. Then Bahá'u'lláh came out and went to the grieving people in the street to comfort them before He left. They began the first stage of this last journey, on the road to Gallipoli.

The Journey to 'Akká

The exiles only stayed a few days in Gallipoli, but those days were painful.

The exiles only stayed a few days in Gallipoli, but those days were painful. The officials there could not seem to decide who was to go where. Sometimes it seemed as if Bahá'u'lláh and His two faithful brothers would be sent to one place, and that His family and the other Bahá'ís would be split up and sent to many other places. This frightened the companions more than anything. Then a rumour was heard that everyone but Bahá'u'lláh would be sent back to Persia, and perhaps killed there.

But at last, after three anxious days of rumour and confusion, everything was settled. The exiles would all stay together, and would be sent to the prison city of 'Akká. Only those exiles whose names were on the government list would be sent with Bahá'u'lláh, but the others were permitted to buy tickets with their own money and go along with Him if they wanted to.

If they wanted to! The few Bahá'ís whose names were not on the list rushed joyfully down to buy their tickets for the steamship. The government officials couldn't believe it. What kind of people would buy their own tickets to prison? The steamer arrived, and the company of believers was taken aboard by little boats. These boats pitched and yawed in the rough sea. 'Would it not be a treat if the liner should sink!' joked Bahá'u'lláh. Then, seeing the alarmed looks on the faces of the companions, He added firmly, 'But it will not sink, even if it is battered by the waves.' So they went on, the steamer stopping at Smyrna, and then Alexandria, where the exiles changed ships. Several of them went ashore to buy fresh food while there was a chance.

Some time before, Nabíl had been sent to Egypt by Bahá'u'lláh to try and help some Bahá'ís who had been put in prison there. But then Nabíl himself had been put into prison. The Bahá'ís had heard of his arrest, but no one knew where in Egypt he was held captive.

As one of the Bahá'ís from the steamer hurried along the roads of Alexandria, he was startled by a familiar voice calling out his name. He looked up and saw Nabíl waving to him from the jailhouse roof. He managed to get in and speak with Nabíl, and told him that Bahá'u'lláh was aboard the steamer in the harbour. Nabíl was beside himself - that Bahá'u'lláh should be so near and yet so far! The jailer came in and said that Nabíl's visitor must go, and so he left, promising to return if he could.

There was another Bahá'í in that prison. He was a doctor, and had been arrested because he owed money and could not pay it. In those days you could be put in prison for being in debt. At the time of his arrest, he had been a Christian. In the prison he had talked to Nabíl often, trying to convert him to Christianity. But the opposite had happened, and the Christian doctor was now a Bahá'í. His name was Fáris, and when he heard the news of Bahá'u'lláh's presence on the ship he was very excited. 'Don't worry', he said to Nabíl. 'We cannot go and see Him, but we can write a letter, can't we?'

The next day a young Christian friend of Fáris, named Constantine, visited the prison. Constantine agreed to take the letters that Nabíl and Fáris had written and deliver them to the ship. Nabíl and Fáris stood on the jail's roof watching as Constantine headed down to the harbour. He disappeared into the crowded streets, and the two prisoners craned their necks after him. Then they heard the ship's hooter sound, and the noise of its engines starting. Had Constantine got there in time? It hardly seemed possible.

The ship slid slowly out of the dock, and then the prisoners saw a tiny rowboat battling through the waves behind it. The ship was drawing near to the mouth of the harbour when suddenly it stopped. The rowboat struggled on, and then they saw the rower hauled aboard. Could it be Constantine? Nabíl and Fáris could hardly keep themselves still as they waited for him to return.

At last he came back, and as he came in the door he exclaimed, 'By God! I saw the Father of Christ.' Fáris took him by the shoulders and kissed his eyes, eyes that had been blessed by seeing Bahá'u'lláh.

Constantine had brought a Tablet from Bahá'u'lláh, a letter from 'Abdu'l-Bahá and a package of almond *nuql* from the Purest Branch. These are clusters of rose-scented sugar with pieces of almond in the middle. *Nuql* are special sweets, usually given out at weddings or New Year. In the Tablet Bahá'u'lláh mentioned Fáris by name, and greatly praised him. Now the prisoners' hearts were full.

They were both to be released from jail soon. Fáris would travel among the Christians, teaching the new Faith, while Nabíl would go to 'Akká. He would camp in Elijah's cave, waiting for the chance to see Bahá'u'lláh again.

Sometimes in 'Akká, as he gazed longingly over at the barracks window, he would see a handkerchief fluttering, and he would know that Bahá'u'lláh was there, waving to him.

A hostile crowd greets the exiles in 'Akká, Palestine

Meanwhile, the steamer went on to Port Said, and then to Jaffa in the Holy Land before arriving at last in Haifa. A sailing boat then took the little group of exiles across the bay to 'Akká. There on the shores, a crowd had gathered to jeer and hurl curses at the 'God of the Persians'. The mullás of 'Akká had read out a list of cruel lies about Bahá'u'lláh in the city's mosques. They had told the people of 'Akká that He was an enemy of the Faith of Islám, a leader of rebellions against the government, and a wicked criminal. They did this to make the people hate Bahá'u'lláh, so that they would not listen to Him.

The exiles waded through heavy waves that lapped against the city wall, and were pushed along through a jostling, angry mob to the fortress of 'Akká, the Most Great Prison.

In this way, the Promised One came to the Holy Land, as all the prophets of the past had said He would. This was the end of all His journeying - the Prison City of 'Akká.

The Most Great Prison

The exiles were marched along narrow streets that wound between grimy stone buildings.

The exiles were marched along narrow streets that wound between grimy stone buildings. The houses seemed to lean over them, blocking out the sunlight. They came to the fortress, and were taken up the steep stairs to their prison cells. The floors of the cells were covered in mud. Shreds of plaster from the ceiling wisped down as the door clanged shut. The day was steaming hot, and hardly any fresh air came into the cells. The heat and the stink of the place were so bad that Bahíyyih Khánum collapsed in a faint.

In that heat they were given no water to drink. For hours the little children of the companions were crying out for water, and for something to eat. The guards would not listen, even though 'Abdu'l-Bahá asked them many times to at least have mercy on those little ones. He even sent a message to the Governor, but there was no answer.

At last, near midnight, the Governor sent a small quantity of water and a little gritty, ill-cooked rice which hardly anyone could stomach. But later that night, when some of the believers were unpacking their belongings, they found a few pieces of good bread, left over and forgotten from their stop in Gallipoli. To their joy, there was also the end of a package of sugar. They soaked the bread, which was now stale, in some of the water, and, with the sugar, made a dish which they hoped Bahá'u'lláh might be able to eat, for He was very ill. When they brought Him the dish, He received it lovingly, but immediately said 'I command you to take this to the children.' Though the dish was not large the children were able to have a few spoonfuls each, enough to let them sleep.

The following morning more water was brought, with some loaves of bitter black bread. This bread was so bad that the weakened children could not keep it down. After some time the prisoners were allowed to exchange the bitter bread for fewer loaves of a better sort. Later on they were given a little money instead of bread, and were allowed to buy food of their own choosing.

The prison was so dirty, and the food so meagre, that soon all but two of the prisoners were desperately ill. Only 'Abdu'l-Bahá and one other Bahá'í were well enough to nurse the others. The jailers would not call a doctor or give them any medicine. All 'Abdu'l-Bahá could do was to cook some broth and soft rice for them, and bathe their faces with the little water He had.

Three of the believers died of this sickness. The first was Abu'l-Qásim-i-Sultán. Then two brothers died in each other's arms as they lay on the rough floor.

The guards came and leaned on the bars of the cell door when they were called. 'Our friends have died,' the grieving Bahá'ís told them, 'and now we must bury their bodies.'
'You can't go out to bury them', retorted the guards. 'We have our orders you know.' When the Bahá'ís begged them to help, the guards lounged off, saying, 'You'll have to pay us well, if you want us to bury them for you.'

But no one had any money. Bahá'u'lláh gave them the only fine thing He had left, a little Persian prayer carpet which He used. They took it, and then carried the bodies out. They buried the three as they were, without washing their bodies or putting them in coffins. The money that they got from selling Bahá'u'lláh's prayer carpet would easily have paid for those things to be done three times over, but the guards just wanted to keep all the money for themselves.

After those deaths, Bahá'u'lláh revealed a short healing prayer, and asked the believers to chant it over and over with sincere hearts. The believers did so, and soon they were all well again.

There in that prison cell Bahá'u'lláh comforted the friends. 'Fear not', He told them. 'These doors shall be opened, My tent shall be pitched on Mount Carmel, and the utmost joy shall be realized.'

Out on the plain beyond 'Akká, Nabíl was wandering, gazing helplessly over the moat at the tiny barred windows of the prison. He could not go into 'Akká, for the soldiers there had recognized him as a Bahá'í. No one who was even suspected of being a Bahá'í was allowed into the barracks to see Bahá'u'lláh.

One day Nabíl was joined in his vigil by another Bahá'í, named 'Abdu'r-Rahím, who had walked all the way from Persia to see Bahá'u'lláh. 'It is not possible', Nabíl told him sadly. 'I have been here for months, and have only seen Him wave to me each day through the bars of that window. If I cannot get in, how can you?' 'Very well', replied 'Abdu'r-Rahím, 'I shall do what I can.' He decided to circle around the prison city, and offer up his prayers to Bahá'u'lláh. Before

doing this he washed his travel-stained clothes in the sea, so as to be clean for his Lord. When he put them on again they looked quite strange, for they had shrunk and were ragged from the long journey. 'Never mind,' 'Abdu'r-Raḥím told himself, 'at least I am clean. He won't mind if I look a bit funny.' So he began walking prayerfully around 'Akká. To his surprise he saw a hand beckoning to him from Bahá'u'lláh's window. He gazed at it in wonder. The hand was most certainly beckoning, not waving.

He rushed to the gates of the prison city, which were always guarded by soldiers. But the soldiers seemed to be frozen into stillness. They didn't even flicker an eyelid as he went past. Feeling like a ghost flitting invisibly through

Nabíl gazes helplessly at the tiny barred windows of Bahá'u'lláh's prison

the city, 'Abdu'r-Raḥím climbed the stairs to the barracks, walked past the guards and into the prison cell where he knelt at Bahá'u'lláh's feet. He was able to stay for some days. Bahá'u'lláh gave him Tablets to deliver to the Bahá'ís of Persia, and he left 'Akká the same way as he had come in. He went back to Persia with the precious Tablets, and told the Bahá'ís of his extraordinary pilgrimage.

At this time there was a religious leader among the Muslims of 'Akká called Sh͟aykh Maḥmúd. When he was a boy an old holy man had come to his father's house, and had told him that he would live to see the Promised One come to 'Akká. He even told Sh͟aykh Maḥmúd that the Lord would speak Persian and would live at the top of a steep flight of steps. But Sh͟aykh Maḥmúd did not think of the holy man's prediction when Bahá'u'lláh came to 'Akká. He had grown up to be a devoted Muslim, and was very angry that this 'God of the Persians' should be in his city. He decided to get rid of this enemy of Islám all by himself.

He hid a weapon carefully under his cloak, and went to the prison. He told the guards that he wanted to see Bahá'u'lláh. Because he was an important religious leader, they agreed, and went to tell Bahá'u'lláh that He had a visitor. Shaykh Maḥmúd waited, smiling to himself and planning what he would do once he got into that cell.

Then the guards came back with a message from Bahá'u'lláh. 'He says', the guards reported, 'that you should throw away your weapon, and then you can come in.'

Shaykh Maḥmúd jumped back in surprise. He looked quickly down at his cloak, but not one bit of the weapon could be seen sticking out. He was very upset, and decided to go home. But after a few days he began to think that he could always kill Bahá'u'lláh with his bare hands. 'I am strong enough, after all', he thought grimly, flexing his fingers.

Back he went, and again asked to see Bahá'u'lláh. Again the guard returned with a message. 'He says that you must purify your heart, and then you can come in.' Shaykh Maḥmúd turned straight around and went back home.

That night he had a dream in which he saw the old holy man again. 'Have you forgotten what I told you about the Promised One?' the old man asked. After this dream Shaykh Maḥmúd went back to the barracks. When he was brought to Bahá'u'lláh he fell down at His feet and humbly begged to be accepted as a believer.

Now that he was a Bahá'í, Shaykh Maḥmúd was able to help pilgrims get into the prison city to see Bahá'u'lláh. Sometimes he lowered ropes over the walls for them to climb. Other times he went out of the city then returned with a Bahá'í pretending to be a servant carrying a lantern in front of his master. No one suspected Shaykh Maḥmúd of being a Bahá'í, so they never checked up on what he was doing. Now, at least, some of the believers were getting through, and taking news and Tablets with them back to Persia, Syria, 'Iráq and Egypt, to the lonely Bahá'ís scattered through those lands.

The Death of Mírzá Mihdí

One evening a splintering crash echoed through the prison.

One evening a splintering crash echoed through the prison. The believers rushed to see what it was, and Bahá'u'lláh came out from His cell anxiously asking what had happened.

Mírzá Mihdí was lying in a shattered crate among jagged spars of wood. One spar was driven through his chest, and a pool of blood was slowly spreading around him.

He had been walking quietly on the roof, as he often did, praying and meditating. As he paced around the little space that evening, he had become so lost in prayer that he forgot where he was and fell through an open skylight.

They carried him gently to his room and a doctor was called, but he said he could not help. The believers gathered around the Purest Branch. He smiled warmly at them, though they could see him breathing carefully because of the pain. 'I am ashamed to be lying down like this while you are all sitting', he remarked.

Then Bahá'u'lláh came into the room and asked the believers to leave Him alone with His son. Then He took Mírzá Mihdí's hand and cradled it in His own. 'Áqá, what do you wish? Tell Me', He asked. Mírzá Mihdí did not think of himself for one moment. He did not ask to be healed and to live, though he well knew that Bahá'u'lláh was able to grant such a wish. He gazed into his Father's tender eyes and said, 'I wish the people of Bahá to be able to attain Your presence.' 'And so it shall be', Bahá'u'lláh said. 'God will grant your wish.' And so, at twenty-two years of age, the Purest Branch died, offering up his life as a sacrifice. From outside the room the believers heard Bahá'u'lláh's voice crying out in grief, 'Mihdí! O Mihdí!'

The roof of the prison where Mirzá Mihdí used to walk

Shaykh Maḥmúd now came to the prison and asked 'Abdu'l-Bahá if he might be allowed to prepare the body of the Purest Branch for burial. 'I do not want the guards to touch his holy body', explained the Shaykh, and 'Abdu'l-Bahá agreed.

A tent was pitched in the barracks courtyard, and there Mírzá Mihdí's body was washed and shrouded by loving hands. It was placed in a casket and carried to a cemetery outside 'Akká. As the casket was lowered into the grave an earth tremor shook the whole of 'Akká for minutes on end.

Navváb could hardly bear the loss of her much-loved younger son. He had been separated from her for most of his childhood. After his death she could not stop crying, for her heart was broken.

But then Bahá'u'lláh told her that Mírzá Mihdí had given his life so that the Bahá'ís would be able to freely visit their Lord once more. Not only that, He said, but the sacrifice of Mírzá Mihdí would eventually bring all mankind to life. Because he gave up his life for the sake of the believers, God would bring all humanity into the Most Great Peace.

When she heard this Navváb was much comforted, and was able to stop crying.

Soon after the death of Mírzá Mihdí the guards relaxed the rules of the prison, and many more pilgrims were able to visit Bahá'u'lláh. Four months later the prisoners were moved out of the barracks into a house in 'Akká. Now the pilgrims could come freely to see Bahá'u'lláh and hear His words. This was the Purest Branch's loving gift to them, a gift which he bought with his life.

In the City

After Bahá'u'lláh and His companions had been living in 'Akká for some time, a new Governor was sent to the prison city.

After Bahá'u'lláh and His companions had been living in 'Akká for some time, a new Governor was sent to the prison city. His name was Aḥmad Big Tawfíq, and he was a good and just man.

When he was sent to 'Akká to be the Governor there, the enemies of the Faith gave him some of Bahá'u'lláh's Writings to read. They thought that he would be angry with Bahá'u'lláh after reading what He had written, but the exact opposite happened. Aḥmad Big Tawfíq immediately saw that only a truly great and holy Man could have written such wonderful Tablets. He came to see the exiles, and met with 'Abdu'l-Bahá. He loved 'Abdu'l-Bahá so much that he sent his own son to Him for lessons. He very much wished to meet Bahá'u'lláh. However, Bahá'u'lláh now spent all His time revealing His Teachings and meeting with the pilgrims. 'Abdu'l-Bahá was the one who met with the officials and other such people. But the Governor begged again and again to see Bahá'u'lláh, and because he was sincere his wish was granted.

He knelt at Bahá'u'lláh's feet and humbly asked, 'Is there any service You require of me?' Bahá'u'lláh looked at him kindly and said that if he wished to do something he should repair the broken aqueduct, so that the people of 'Akká could have fresh water to drink. 'It is done!' cried Aḥmad Big, and he began the repair work straight away.

Bahá'u'lláh was now living in the house of 'Abbúd, and most of the Bahá'ís had been able to find work in the city. During this peaceful time while Aḥmad Big ruled the city, Bahá'u'lláh revealed the *Kitáb-i-Aqdas*, His book of laws. The Bahá'ís were now ready to accept the new laws given by Bahá'u'lláh. The time had come for them to give up the laws of the Báb which had made them ready for Bahá'u'lláh, and to move on to the new laws which would bring peace to the whole world.

When the authorities saw that the Governor of 'Akká had come to love Bahá'u'lláh, they called him back and sent out a new Governor. This Governor was 'Abdu'r-Raḥmán, and he was a greedy, bullying sort of man. He tried to get the Bahá'ís to pay him bribes, and when they wouldn't pay he sent an angry report to the government in Constantinople.

'These Bahá'ís are not living as prisoners!' he complained. 'They walk around freely in the city, and some of them even own shops!'

Back came the order from the Grand Vizier in Constantinople, 'They are prisoners and have no right to own shops.'

'Abdu'r-Raḥmán was delighted. He went to see one of the religious leaders of 'Akká, a man called S͟haykh 'Alíy-i-Mírí. 'Look at this order from the Grand Vizier', gloated 'Abdu'r-Raḥmán. 'Now I'm going to get these Bahá'ís - I'll send soldiers to wait outside their shops early tomorrow morning and arrest them when they come to open up!'

But the new Governor did not know that S͟haykh 'Alíy-i-Mírí was a good friend of 'Abdu'l-Bahá. He listened quietly to 'Abdu'r-Raḥmán. When he left, the S͟haykh went straight to 'Abdu'l-Bahá and told Him of the Governor's plan. 'You must give him a bribe!' said the S͟haykh. 'It's the only way to stop him.'

'Abdu'l-Bahá did not agree with that idea. He told the S͟haykh to leave everything in God's hands and not to worry. Then He went to see Bahá'u'lláh. Bahá'u'lláh said that the Bahá'ís should not open their shops the next morning. All the Bahá'ís were told, and the next day none of their shops were opened.

The Governor's soldiers waited and waited at the Bahá'ís' shops, but the Bahá'ís did not come. They were all at Bahá'u'lláh's house, wondering what was going to happen next.

In the middle of the morning there came a knock at the door. It was the man from the telegraph office, and he looked very excited. He asked to see 'Abdu'l-Bahá. One of the believers went to get Him, for He was with Bahá'u'lláh. When the message was given Bahá'u'lláh smiled and said, 'Go downstairs Áqá! He has good news. No one can frustrate God in His purpose.'

'Abdu'l-Bahá went down and the man showed Him a telegram which had just come, saying that 'Abdu'r-Raḥmán was removed from the position of Governor.

The Governors who came after 'Abdu'r-Raḥmán were friendly, and made no trouble for the believers. More and more people came to respect and love Bahá'u'lláh. Some of them only had to see Him to realize His greatness. Once, when He was walking to Mírzá Músá's house, He passed a coffee shop where the new officer in charge of customs was sitting with his assistants. To their own surprise, the officer and all his assistants found themselves rising to their

Mazra'ih, where Bahá'u'lláh was allowed to live after leaving prison

feet and bowing to Him. He greeted them lovingly and passed on. The officer turned in bewilderment to his friends and asked, 'Is this the Holy Spirit or the King of Kings? Who is He?'

'He is the Father of 'Abbás Effendi', they all replied.

One day at about this time Bahá'u'lláh remarked, 'I have not gazed on greenery for nine years. The country is the world of the soul, the city is the world of bodies.'

When 'Abdu'l-Bahá heard about this remark, He felt sure that Bahá'u'lláh was longing for the open countryside. He went out and rented the mansion of Mazra'ih, which was some miles from the city.

Mazra'ih was a large gracious house, set amongst gardens and orchards. A stream ran through the gardens, chattering to itself among the orange trees.

When the house was made ready, 'Abdu'l-Bahá went to His Father and said,

'The mansion at Mazra'ih is ready for You, and a carriage to drive You there.' But Bahá'u'lláh refused to go, saying, 'I am a prisoner.'

Later on 'Abdu'l-Bahá tried again, but was given the same answer. He even asked a third time, but Bahá'u'lláh said, 'No!' and 'Abdu'l-Bahá did not dare ask any more. So He went to His friend, Shaykh 'Alíy-i-Mírí, and said, 'You are daring. Go tonight to Bahá'u'lláh, fall on your knees before Him, take hold of His hands and do not let go until He promises to leave the city!'

That night Shaykh 'Alíy-i-Mírí, the religious leader of 'Akká, went to Bahá'u'lláh and knelt beside Him. He took hold of Bahá'u'lláh's hands and kissed them, asking, 'Why do you not want to leave the city?'
'I am a prisoner', replied Bahá'u'lláh.

'God forbid!' exclaimed the Shaykh. 'Who has the power to make You a prisoner? You have kept Yourself in prison. It was Your own will to be imprisoned, and now I beg You to come out and go to Mazra'ih. It is so beautiful and green there! The trees are lovely, and the oranges are like balls of fire!'

Every time Bahá'u'lláh said, 'I am a prisoner, it cannot be', the Shaykh took His hands and kissed them. He pleaded with Bahá'u'lláh in this way for a whole hour, and at last Bahá'u'lláh said, 'Very good.'

The next day the carriage was brought, and Bahá'u'lláh was driven out to Mazra'ih. None of the government officials said a word about His departure. The prison doors had opened wide.

Mazra'ih and Bahjí

Now the pilgrims came to see Bahá'u'lláh in the fresh air of Mazra'ih.

Now the pilgrims came to see Bahá'u'lláh in the fresh air of Mazra'ih. They walked in freedom through the green meadows and orchards with Him, listening to Him speak.

Once He was heard to say, 'There are four qualities which I love to see in people: first, enthusiasm and courage; second, a face wreathed in smiles; third, that they see all things with their own eyes and not through the eyes of others; fourth, the ability to carry a task, once begun, through to its end.'

One of the Bahá'ís who came on pilgrimage at this time was Ḥájí Mírzá Ḥaydar-'Alí. He was so happy to be with Bahá'u'lláh that he couldn't bear to leave. When the end of his pilgrimage came he begged 'Abdu'l-Bahá to speak for him, and to ask Bahá'u'lláh for permission to stay two more weeks. Bahá'u'lláh gave him permission to stay a whole month more. Ḥaydar-'Alí was very happy. But eventually the last day of that extra month came. That night Bahá'u'lláh sent Ḥaydar-'Alí some sweets as a gift. A message came with the sweets. 'Tell him', Bahá'u'lláh had said, 'to eat the sweets and say to himself, "I must go home".' Ḥaydar-'Alí still felt sad about leaving, but every time he looked at the sweets he had to laugh, and this cheered his heart.

The next morning came with a torrent of rain, so that travel was impossible. Bahá'u'lláh looked at Ḥaydar-'Alí with twinkling eyes and said, 'It seems that you expect the rain to intercede for you.'

Then He spoke to Ḥaydar-'Alí about teaching the Faith. He said, 'Consideration, respect and love encourage people to listen and do not force them to respond with hostility. They are convinced because they see that your purpose is not to defeat them, but to convey truth, to manifest courtesy, and to show forth heavenly attributes. This will encourage the people to be fair. Their spiritual natures will respond, and, by the bounty of God, they will find themselves recreated.'

A few years later a larger house became available. The people who lived there had all died or run away because of a dangerous epidemic. 'Abdu'l-Bahá was able to rent this house called Bahjí, which means 'Place of Delight'.

When Bahá'u'lláh moved there, the Bahá'ís of 'Akká would come each Friday to see Him. They would bring their children with them and stay all day. During

Bahá'u'lláh has placed a cake on Áqá Muḥammad's head

one of these visits, when the grown-ups were all having their afternoon sleep, one of the children grew bored. It was hot, and he couldn't sleep. His name was Áqá Muḥammad, and he was only four years old.

Áqá Muḥammad decided to go for a walk around the mansion, and set off down the cool hallway, peering into doors as he went. It was very quiet. He came to the pantry, and went in to look at all the jars and bags of stored food. Up on a shelf he found a bag of rock sugar, like lumps of candy. He took one handful and put it in his mouth, and then filled both hands before leaving the pantry to run back to his parents.

As he trotted back down the hall he saw a grown-up pacing there, and then froze into stillness as he realized that it was Bahá'u'lláh Himself!

Bahá'u'lláh slowly walked towards him. The little boy quickly put his hands behind his back, and gazed wide-eyed up at Him as He approached. Then Bahá'u'lláh gently led him over to a big table in the middle of the hall, where there was a plate full of sweet cakes. Bahá'u'lláh took the plate, and lovingly offered it to Áqá Muḥammad. What could he do? Both hands were still clenched stickily behind his back!

Bahá'u'lláh laughed, took one of the cakes and gently balanced it on the little boy's head. 'It seems you like sweets', He said. 'Eat well! Goodbye. And may God protect you.'

'Abdu'l-Bahá had also been able to buy a garden which lay between two streams. This garden had been planted with flowers, fragrant herbs and fruit trees brought from Persia by the pilgrims. Bahá'u'lláh named it the Riḍván Garden, in memory of the garden outside Baghdád where He had first declared His Mission. At the centre of the garden stood two tall, shady mulberry trees. Benches had been set out beneath them for everyone to sit on. A little fountain played nearby, and the sound of its splashing was a refreshment in itself.

Sometimes Bahá'u'lláh would take His grandchildren there for picnics. He often called them to Him when they were being taken off to bed and being told not to bother Him. 'Let the dear children come in, and have some dessert', He would say.

If a picnic was planned, He would wait until they were all clustered around Him and say, 'Now children, tomorrow you shall come with Me for a picnic to the Riḍván Garden.' That night the children would hardly be able to sleep for thinking about the treat to come.

The Riḍván Garden was cared for by Bahá'u'lláh's faithful gardener, 'Abu'l-Qásim. Bahá'u'lláh would often tell him, 'This is the most beautiful garden in the world.'

One hot summer 'Abu'l-Qásim had been working out in the garden when he saw a thick brown cloud of locusts whirring towards the garden. He knew that locusts can chew all the greenery off a garden in a matter of hours. In moments the locusts had covered the tall mulberry trees which Bahá'u'lláh loved to sit beneath.

'Abu'l-Qásim ran to Bahá'u'lláh. 'My Lord!' he gasped, 'The locusts have come, and are eating away the shade from above Thy blessed head. I beg of Thee to cause them to depart.' Bahá'u'lláh smiled, and said, 'The locusts must be fed; let them be.' 'Abu'l-Qásim went back into the garden and watched in agitation as the locusts chewed away at the smooth, dark green leaves. But he could not bear it. He went back and begged Bahá'u'lláh to send the locusts away.

Bahá'u'lláh came out into the garden and stood under the rustling trees. He said, 'Abu'l-Qásim does not want you; God protect you.' Then He lifted the hem of His robe and shook it. All the locusts rose up from the trees together and gathered into a thick brown cloud again. Then they all flew away.

In despair the gardener, Abu'l-Qásim, sees the locusts arriving in the garden

The Death of Navváb

One day when Bahá'u'lláh's grandchildren came back from school, they found many people in the house.

One day when Bahá'u'lláh's grandchildren came back from school, they found many people in the house. They all looked very serious, and stood around talking quietly to each other in the hall.
'What is the matter?' asked the children.
'Your grandmother is very ill', they were told.

They waited with the grown-ups, being as quiet as they could. Some of them thought of how unselfish Navváb had been all her life. Whenever anyone was ill, she was there to nurse and comfort them. They thought of her ready laugh, and of how she always listened to them and understood their little difficulties. It was hard to think that they would not see her sweet, smiling face again.

Jasmine flowers

Bahá'u'lláh went into Navváb's room. He stayed with her until she died. When they heard that she had truly gone the children wept aloud. But the grown-ups told them that Navváb's life had been so filled with suffering that they should be glad that she was free at last.

After her death Bahá'u'lláh wrote a Tablet saying that she would always be His beloved companion, in all the worlds of God. He revealed a special prayer for the Bahá'ís to say at her resting place. This prayer says in part:

'We pray God that He may forgive us, and forgive them that have turned unto thee (Navváb), and grant their desires, and bestow upon them, through His wondrous grace, whatever be their wish.'

By saying this prayer at her shrine the believers can still turn to Navváb, and ask for her gentle help in all their troubles.

The Shrines of Bahá'u'lláh's wife, Navváb, and of His son, Mírzá Mihdí

The Last Days

During the last years of His life Bahá'u'lláh devoted Himself to revealing teachings and prayers.

During the last years of His life Bahá'u'lláh devoted Himself to revealing teachings and prayers. The Bahá'ís were allowed to see Him, but all other visitors were sent to 'Abdu'l-Bahá.

One visitor, however, was allowed to see Him. He was a professor named Edward Granville Browne, and he had come all the way from Cambridge University in England, hoping to see Bahá'u'lláh.

After staying one night in Bahjí, he was taken upstairs and shown into Bahá'u'lláh's room. He saw Bahá'u'lláh sitting quietly in the corner where the divan met the wall. He later said, 'The face of Him on Whom I gazed I can never forget, though I cannot describe it. Those piercing eyes seemed to read one's very soul...'

Edward Granville Browne bowed his head in awe, and heard a gentle, dignified voice asking him to be seated.

He listened to the words of Bahá'u'lláh there in the stillness of that quiet room.

'Thou hast come to see a Prisoner and an Exile... We desire but the good of the world and the happiness of the nations; yet they deem us a stirrer up of strife and sedition worthy of bondage and banishment... That all nations should become one in Faith and all men as brothers... What harm is there in this?'

As He spoke, the professor's heart filled with wonder. These were ideas that were unusual at the time. Bahá'u'lláh went on, *'Yet so it shall be; these fruitless strifes, these ruinous wars shall pass away, and the Most Great Peace shall come.'*

Edward Granville Browne wrote of his visit to Bahá'u'lláh in one of his books. He quoted the words of Bahá'u'lláh that he had heard, and asked his readers to think for themselves if it was right for the authorities to imprison and banish Bahá'u'lláh for teaching such wonderful ideas.

Soon after Edward Granville Browne's visit Bahá'u'lláh was able to go to Haifa and stay there for some time. He pitched His tent on Mount Carmel, and now His prophecy in the prison barracks was completely fulfilled. The doors of the prison had opened, and He had pitched His tent on Carmel, just as He said He would.

One day, when He was walking out on the wild mountainside with 'Abdu'l-Bahá, He stopped in the shade of a stand of cypress trees. They had climbed almost halfway up the rocky slopes of the mountain. Bahá'u'lláh pointed down at an outcrop of rocks below and told 'Abdu'l-Bahá that this was the place where the Shrine of the Báb was to be built.

Today on that very spot the Shrine stands, all white and gold amongst roses, jacaranda and crimson, tumbling bougainvillea. Thousands of pilgrims now come each year to pray at that Shrine, and to walk in the Gardens of Carmel.

The cypress trees on Mount Carmel where Bahá'u'lláh stood and pointed out where the Shrine of the Báb should be built

The Passing of Bahá'u'lláh

About nine months before His passing, Bahá'u'lláh spoke of His wish to leave this world.

About nine months before His passing, Bahá'u'lláh spoke of His wish to leave this world. The friends saw from the way He was making ready that the end of His life was drawing near. They realized that He was preparing them for the time when He would be gone.

He would often speak to the Bahá'ís about 'Abdu'l-Bahá. He told Ḥaydar-'Alí that 'Abdu'l-Bahá's power was hidden now but that soon it would be clearly seen. He said that 'Abdu'l-Bahá would, alone and unaided, 'hold aloft the banner of the Most Great Name in all the ends of the earth.'

'Abdu'l-Bahá was still living in 'Akká with His family at this time. One day a servant rode in from Bahjí with a message from Bahá'u'lláh. He had said, 'I am

One of Bahá'u'lláh's grandchildren, little Rúḥangíz, rushing ahead to visit Bahá'u'lláh in the mansion of Bahjí

not well, come to Me and bring <u>Kh</u>ánum.' <u>Kh</u>ánum was Bahíyyih <u>Kh</u>ánum, Bahá'u'lláh's daughter.

'Abdu'l-Bahá and His sister went to Bahjí at once. It seemed that Bahá'u'lláh had a kind of malaria. Days went by and the fever grew worse. On the fifteenth day of His illness He asked to see the Bahá'ís of 'Akká and the pilgrims.

They came into His room and gathered round Him weeping. He lay in bed leaning against one of His sons. 'I am well pleased with you all', He gently told them. 'Ye have rendered many services, and been very assiduous in your labours. Ye have come here every morning and every evening. May God assist you to remain united. May He aid you to exalt the Cause of the Lord of Being.'

When the believers heard these words they knew that the end had come. A believer named Ismá'íl was so heartbroken that he stood and cried aloud, with tears running down his face. Bahá'u'lláh told him to come nearer, so he came and knelt by the bed. Bahá'u'lláh took His handkerchief and wiped Ismá'íl's cheeks, drying his tears.

He told the believers that they must now depend on 'Abdu'l-Bahá, and that all arrangements for the Holy Family, the believers and the Cause of God had been left in His hands.

On the day of Bahá'u'lláh's passing from this world the plain between 'Akká and Bahjí was filled with crowds who came to mourn Him. There were government officials and religious leaders, poets and professors, rich men and poor. From other cities letters of tribute and poems praising Him came - and these were not His followers, but people who had come to know Him, and so to love Him. The grief of the Bahá'ís themselves was beyond measuring. From Persia, India, Russia, 'Iráq, Turkey, Palestine, Egypt and Syria letters poured in from the Bahá'ís, telling of their sorrow and their determination to follow Bahá'u'lláh's teachings and to spread His Faith.

One of His grandchildren was especially sad after Bahá'u'lláh's death. When she had been born, some people had remarked that it was a great pity that she was not a boy. Bahá'u'lláh had said, 'I will love her more than all the rest; you must not wish that she had been a boy.'

This little girl, Rúḥangíz, loved Bahá'u'lláh with her whole heart. When He passed away, she could not understand why she could not be with Him any more. 'Where is He?' she asked. They told her that He had gone away, through a door into Heaven.
'I want to go through that same door to Heaven', she said firmly. They explained to her that only Bahá'u'lláh could decide if she might go through or not, and that she must live her life as He would have wished. But she only longed to be with her beloved Grandfather. 'No thank you', she would say, 'I do not wish for anything. I would like best of all to go to Him.'

After a year had gone by, her wish was granted. She fell ill, and left this world. Bahá'u'lláh had opened the door and let her through to be with Him again.

The Covenant

Bahá'u'lláh promised the Bahá'ís that He would always be with them, even after His death.

Bahá'u'lláh promised the Bahá'ís that He would always be with them, even after His death. He said, 'We are with you at all times, and shall strengthen you through the power of truth.'

The believers remembered how He had always seen into their hearts, no matter how far away from Him they were.

Once, a believer named Na'ím had been reading one of Bahá'u'lláh's books in Persia. In that book he found a prayer that he loved more than any other. As he read it, he found himself wishing that it could have been written especially for him. Then he sadly put the book down, saying to himself that he was unworthy of such an honour in any case.

A few months later Na'ím received a Tablet from Bahá'u'lláh. In those days letters took at least three months to get from 'Akká to Persia. Na'ím realized that the Tablet from Bahá'u'lláh must have been sent at just the time when he wished for that special prayer to be his.

He opened the letter and found that Bahá'u'lláh had revealed that same prayer a second time, but in Na'ím's name! Bahá'u'lláh said in His letter that now the prayer had been revealed again especially for Na'ím, he must chant it very beautifully, for he was one of those who had been given their heart's desire.

Now that Bahá'u'lláh had passed into the next world, the believers remembered this story, and others like it. They knew that He was still watching over them, and could still hear their prayers and comfort their grieving hearts.

They also knew that He had promised that His Faith would, 'gather together the whole of mankind beneath its shelter.' This now was the task set before His faithful followers. They knew that with His loving help they would be able to spread His teachings through every country of the earth, for He had promised them that this would happen.

But Bahá'u'lláh had left His followers something else. He left them One Who would guide them and care for them just as He had always done. In His Will He appointed 'Abdu'l-Bahá as the Centre of the Covenant. He told the Bahá'ís to take all their difficulties to 'Abdu'l-Bahá, and to obey Him absolutely.

The táj of Bahá'u'lláh on the mandar in His bedroom in Bahjí

This was His Covenant, or agreement, with the believers. He agreed to give them His guidance through 'Abdu'l-Bahá, and they agreed to obey 'Abdu'l-Bahá absolutely.

By this Covenant the unity of the Bahá'í Faith was maintained. 'Abdu'l-Bahá later told the Bahá'ís, 'Thank God that Bahá'u'lláh has made the pathway straight. He has clearly explained all things and opened every door for advancing souls... The purpose of the Covenant was simply to ward off disunion and differences so that no one might say, "My opinion is the true and valid one".'

If there had been no Centre of the Covenant to guide the believers, then some might have followed this opinion, and others that opinion, and they would have split into sects like all the religions of the past. But because they were obedient to 'Abdu'l-Bahá, the Bahá'í Faith remained one Faith, with no divisions in it.

Bahá'u'lláh's Resting Place

Perhaps one day you will visit Bahjí, the Shrine of Bahá'u'lláh.

183

Perhaps one day you will visit Bahjí, the Shrine of Bahá'u'lláh. If you do you will be able to say prayers in His room in the mansion, the room where He spoke with Edward Granville Browne. You will be able to walk under the tall, shady trees of the gardens, between olive groves and roses. And you will walk down the avenue lined with urns. On each urn a cherub perches, finger held softly to his lips. Then you will step into the Holy Shrine itself, where a living garden thrives. Bahá'u'lláh always loved green and growing things.

'Abdu'l-Bahá said of His Father: 'During all His lifetime He had no moment's rest! He did not pass one night in restful sleep for His body!

'He bore all these ordeals and catastrophes and difficulties in order that, in the world of humanity, a selflessness might become apparent. In order that the Most Great Peace might become a reality...'

By learning about Bahá'u'lláh's life and His teachings, studying His Writings and teaching His Faith, we can help to make the Most Great Peace a reality. That is the task set before us, in our day.

Glossary	188
Some Important Dates	191
References	194
Bibliography	198
A Guide to Pronunciation	199

Glossary

Ambassador - An ambassador is an important representative sent from one government to another.

Áqá - This is a title that means sir or master.

Aqueduct - An aqueduct is a raised open channel built especially to carry water from one place to another. The aqueduct that was repaired at the request of Bahá'u'lláh was called the Aqueduct of Sulaymán Páshá and had originally been built in 1815.

Barracks - A barracks is a building where soldiers live. The Most Great Prison in 'Akká was a military barracks and it was only when the authorities needed more housing space for soldiers that Bahá'u'lláh and His companions were moved to a house in the prison city itself.

Big - This is a Turkish word meaning 'prince' or 'lord'. It was used as a title after a man's name.

Calligraphy - Beautiful handwriting. It is sometimes used in Persian and Arabic to turn words into beautiful shapes or pictures.

Caravanserai - These were inns built around large inner courtyards for travellers to stay in.

Consul - A consul is an officer sent by a government to represent it in a particular town or area of a foreign country.

Dervish - A dervish is a Muslim who lives as a travelling religious beggar, giving up all his material possessions to meditate and try to become closer to God.

Effendi - This is a Turkish word which means 'sir' or is a respectful way of saying 'mister'. It is used on its own or placed after someone's name.

Envoy - An envoy is a special messenger sent from one government to another.

Some Important Dates

1817: On the 12th of November, Bahá'u'lláh is born in Ṭihrán.

1835: In October of this year, Bahá'u'lláh marries Ásíyih Khánum, whom He called Navváb.

1844: The Báb declares that He is the Promised One of Islám on the 23rd May.

A few months later, Mullá Ḥusayn reaches Ṭihrán with a letter from the Báb which is given to Bahá'u'lláh. Bahá'u'lláh embraces the new Faith.

1847: The Báb receives a letter and gifts from Bahá'u'lláh.

1848: In the early summer, the conference of Bábís at Badasht takes place.

From October of this year until May 1849, the Bábí defenders are under siege at Fort Ṭabarsí. Bahá'u'lláh is captured and bastinadoed while attempting to join them.

1850: On July the 9th at noon, the Báb is executed by firing squad in the Barracks Square in Tabríz.

1851: Bahá'u'lláh arrives at Karbilá in 'Iráq and meets Shaykh Ḥasan.

1852: An attempt is made on the life of the Sháh on the 15th of August.

Bahá'u'lláh is arrested and imprisoned in the Síyáh-Chál from August-December.

1853: Bahá'u'lláh and His family are exiled from Persia on January 12th, arriving in Baghdád on the 8th of April.

1854: Bahá'u'lláh goes into retreat in the mountains of Kurdistán on the 10th of April.

1856: Bahá'u'lláh returns to Baghdád on the 19th of March. It is here that He reveals the *Hidden Words*, *Seven Valleys* and *Kitáb-i-Iqán*.

1863: The Sultán of the Ottoman Empire invites Bahá'u'lláh to Constantinople.

On April 22nd, 1863, in the Riḍván Garden in Baghdád, Bahá'u'lláh declares Himself to be the Promised One spoken of by the Báb as 'He Whom God will make manifest'.

On May 3rd, Bahá'u'lláh, His family and chosen companions leave Baghdád.

On August 16th, they arrive in Constantinople, leaving that city for further exile on December 1st.

On December 12th, Bahá'u'lláh, accompanied by family and other companions, arrives in Adrianople.

1866: In the spring of 1866, Bahá'u'lláh and His younger half-brother Mírzá Yaḥyá break off all further relationship with each other. This is known by Bahá'ís as the 'Most Great Separation'.

1868: Due mostly to intrigue and lies spread by Mírzá Yaḥyá and his followers, Bahá'u'lláh is banished again, this time to the prison city of 'Akká in Palestine. The Holy Family and their companions leave Adrianople on the 12th of August and arrive at their new place of imprisonment on the 31st of August.

1869: Bahá'u'lláh's chosen messenger, Badí', is sent to the Sháh in Persia with a letter from Bahá'u'lláh. This letter is known as the 'Tablet to the Sháh'. Badí' was tortured and killed after delivering the letter.

1870: On June 23rd, Bahá'u'lláh's twenty-two-year-old son, Mírzá Mihdí, whom He named the 'Purest Branch', died of his injuries after he fell through a skylight in the 'Most Great Prison' in 'Akká.

In October, Bahá'u'lláh and His family are moved out of the prison itself into the House of Malik in 'Akká. Most of His companions are moved to a caravanserai nearby.

1871: The Holy Family moves to the House of 'Udí Khammár, and two years later acquires the use of the adjoining House of 'Abbúd.

1873: Bahá'u'lláh reveals the *Kitáb-i-Aqdas*, the *Most Holy Book*.

1875: 'Abdu'l-Bahá rents a garden near 'Akká, which Bahá'u'lláh names the 'Riḍván Garden'.

1877: Bahá'u'lláh moves to Mazra'ih in June with some of His family. Navváb, 'Abdu'l-Bahá and Bahíyyih Khánum stay on at the House of 'Abbúd.

1879: Bahá'u'lláh moves to the Mansion of Bahjí in September.

1886: Navváb, wife of Bahá'u'lláh for over fifty years and entitled by Him the 'Most Exalted Leaf', dies.

1890: In April, the well-known Cambridge orientalist, Edward Granville Brown, visits Bahá'u'lláh at Bahjí.

During this year, Bahá'u'lláh twice pitches His tent on Mount Carmel and stays for a time.

1892: On May 29th, at 3 a.m., Bahá'u'lláh passes to the Abhá Kingdom. He is 74 years old at the time of His Ascension.

References

Chapter 1:
Story of scholar, pp.3-4 : *Stories of Bahá'u'lláh*, p.4

Chapter 2:
'The Puppet Show', pp.6-8 : *The Summons of the Lord of Hosts*, pp.166-167

Chapter 3:
'Prayer for Peace', p.12 : *Revelation of Bahá'u'lláh*, vol. 2, pp.347-348

Chapter 4:
Comment of Mírzá Buzurg, p.14 : *Stories of Bahá'u'lláh*, p.2

Chapter 5:
Comments of Bahá'u'lláh's friends, p. 22 : *Promulgation of Universal Peace*, pp. 25-26

Chapter 6:
Words of the Báb, p.24 : *Chosen Highway*, p.22
Mullá Ḥusayn's conversation with Mullá Muḥammad, pp.25-27 : *Dawnbreakers*, pp.104-108

Chapter 7:
Words of Ṭáhirih, pp.30-31 : *Dawnbreakers*, p.284
Words of Bahá'u'lláh, p.32 : *Revelation of Bahá'u'lláh*, vol. 2, p.177
Words of Bahá'u'lláh, p.33 : *Revelation of Bahá'u'lláh*, vol. 2, p.178
Comments of Ṭáhirih's relatives, p.33 : *Dawnbreakers*, p.285

Chapter 8:
Words of Quddús and Ṭáhirih, p.37 : *Dawnbreakers*, pp.294-297
Words of Ṭáhirih, p.38 : *Ṭáhirih the Pure*, p.45
Quarrel of Quddús and Ṭáhirih, pp.36-38 : *Dawnbreakers*, p.297

Chapter 9:
Words of villagers fictionalized, p.44 : *Dawnbreakers*, p.299
Words of Bahá'u'lláh's enemies, p.45 : *Dawnbreakers*, p.299
Words of Bahá'u'lláh, p.45 : *Dawnbreakers*, p.300

Chapter 10:
Words of mullás, p.50 : *King of Glory*, p.57
Words of mullás, p.50 : *King of Glory*, p.58
Words of acting Governor, p.50 : *King of Glory*, p.59
Words of Bahá'u'lláh, p.51 : *Stories of Bahá'u'lláh*, p.7
Words of Governor, p.52 : *King of Glory*, p.59

Chapter 12:
Words of Grand Vizier, pp.58-59 : *King of Glory*, p.66
Words of the Báb, p.60 : *Stories of Bahá'u'lláh*, p.9
Words of Bahá'u'lláh, p.60 : *Stories of Bahá'u'lláh*, p.9

Chapter 13:
Words of Russian Ambassador, p.64 : *Dawnbreakers*, p.603
Words of Bahá'u'lláh, p.65 : *King of Glory*, p.78

Chapter 14:
Words of official, p.69 : *Stories of Bahá'u'lláh*, p.12-13
Words of Bahá'u'lláh, p.70 : *Stories of Bahá'u'lláh*, p.14

Chapter 15:
Words of 'Aẓím, p.72 : *Dawnbreakers*, pp.636-637
Words of Russian Ambassador, pp.72-73 : *Chosen Highway*, pp.43-44
Grand Vizier's conversation with Bahá'u'lláh, p.73 : *Dawnbreakers*, pp.648-649

Chapter 17:
Words of Mírzá Yaḥyá, p.86 : *Revelation of Bahá'u'lláh*, vol.1, p.247
Words of Siyyid Muḥammad, pp.87-88 : *Revelation of Bahá'u'lláh*, vol.1, p.54
Words of Mírzá Yaḥyá, p.88 : *Revelation of Bahá'u'lláh*, vol.1, p.55

Chapter 18:
Bahá'u'lláh's conversation with Kurdish boy, p.92 : *Chosen Highway*, p.54
Words of Bahá'u'lláh, p.93 : *Chosen Highway*, p.55

Chapter 19:
Words of Bahá'u'lláh, p.96 : *King of Glory*, p.151
Words of Áqá Siyyid Mujtahid, p.100 : *Chosen Highway*, p.56
Words of Bahá'u'lláh, p.97 : *God Passes By*, p.135
Story of Riḍá Turk, pp.99-100 : *King of Glory*, p.137 and 148

Chapter 20:
Mírzá Yaḥyá's thoughts, p.102 : *King of Glory*, p.158
Words of Little boy, p.103 : *Revelation of Bahá'u'lláh*, vol 1, p.260
Words of Bahá'u'lláh to Mírzá Asadu'lláh, p.106 : *Revelation of Bahá'u'lláh*, vol. 1, p.302

Chapter 21:
Words of Bahá'u'lláh, p.110 : *Chosen Highway*, p.59
Words of Persian Official, p.110 : *Chosen Highway*, p.59

Words of Persian Ambassador, p.111 : *God Passes By*, p.159
Words of Grand Vizier, p.112 : *Stories of Bahá'u'lláh*, p.37

Chapter 22:
Words of believers, p.116 : *Revelation of Bahá'u'lláh*, vol. 2, pp.67-69
Words of Bahá'u'lláh, p.120 : Revelation of Bahá'u'lláh, vol. 2, p.111

Chapter 23:
Words of Dr Shishmán, pp.122-123 : *King of Glory*, p.225
Words of Bahá'u'lláh, p.123 : *King of Glory*, p.226

Chapter 24:
Words of Bahá'u'lláh, p.126 : *King of Glory*, p.244
Words of Badí', p.127 : *King of Glory*, p.300
Words of Napoleon III, p.129 : *Bahá'u'lláh*, by Balyuzi, p.43
Words of Queen Victoria, p.130 : *Bahá'u'lláh*, by Balyuzi, p.51

Chapter 25:
Words of Bahá'u'lláh, p.132 : *King of Glory*, p.235
Words of Bahá'u'lláh, p.132 : *Delight of Hearts*, p.22
Words of Mírzá Yahyá, p.132 : *Delight of Hearts*, p.22
Words of Bahá'u'lláh, p.132 : *Delight of Hearts*, p.23

Chapter 26:
Words of Bahá'u'lláh, p.138 : *King of Glory*, p.264
Words of Fáris, p.139 : *King of Glory*, p.267
Words of Constantine, p.139 : *King of Glory*, p.268

Chapter 27:
Words of Bahá'u'lláh, p.144 : *The Master in 'Akká*, p.81
Words of guards, p.145 : *Revelation of Bahá'u'lláh*, vol. 3, p.20
Words of Bahá'u'lláh, p.145 : *King of Glory*, p.360
Words of Nabíl and 'Abdu'r-Rahím, p.145 : *Revelation of Bahá'u'lláh*, vol. 3, p.60
Reported words of Bahá'u'lláh, p.148 : *Revelation of Bahá'u'lláh*, vol. 3, p.67

Chapter 28:
Words of Mírzá Mihdí, p.150 : *Revelation of Bahá'u'lláh*, vol. 3, p.207
Words of Bahá'u'lláh, pp.150-151 : *King of Glory*, p.311
Words of Shaykh Mahmúd, p.152 : *King of Glory*, p.313

Chapter 29:
Words of Ahmad Big Tawfíq, p.154 : *King of Glory*, p.334
Words of 'Abdu'r-Rahmán, p.154 : *Revelation of Bahá'u'lláh*, vol. 3, p.410
Words of Shaykh 'Alíy-i-Mírí, p.155 : *Revelation of Bahá'u'lláh*, vol. 3, p.411

Words of Bahá'u'lláh, p.155 : *Delight of Hearts*, p.71
Words of Bahá'u'lláh, pp.155-156 : *Bahá'í Holy Places*, p.29
Conversation between 'Abdu'l-Bahá and Bahá'u'lláh, p.157 : *Bahá'í Holy Places*, p.30
Conversation between 'Abdu'l-Bahá and <u>Sh</u>ay<u>kh</u>, p.158 : *Bahá'í Holy Places*, p.30

Chapter 30:
Words of Bahá'u'lláh, p.160 : *Stories of Bahá'u'lláh*, p.51
Words of Bahá'u'lláh, p.160 : *Delight of Hearts*, p.109
Words of Bahá'u'lláh, p.160 : *Delight of Hearts*, p.109
Words of Bahá'u'lláh on teaching, p.160 : *Delight of Hearts*, p.109
Words of Bahá'u'lláh, p.162 : *Stories of Bahá'u'lláh*, p.69
Words of Bahá'u'lláh, p.162 : *Chosen Highway*, p.98
Words of Bahá'u'lláh, p.162 : *Revelation of Bahá'u'lláh*, vol. 4, p.29

Chapter 31:
Prayer for Navváb's shrine, p.168 : *Bahá'í Holy Places*, p.77

Chapter 32:
Visit of Edward Granville Browne, p.172 : *King of Glory*, pp.371-373

Chapter 33:
Words of Bahá'u'lláh, p.176 : *Stories of Bahá'u'lláh*, p.77
Bahá'u'lláh's message, p.176 : *Chosen Highway*, p.105
Words of Bahá'u'lláh to believers, p.177 : *Stories of Bahá'u'lláh*, p.108
Words of Bahá'u'lláh, p.178 : *Chosen Highway*, p.103
Words of Rúḥangíz, p.178 : *Chosen Highway*, p.103

Chapter 34:
Words of Bahá'u'lláh, p.180 : *Revelation of Bahá'u'lláh*, vol. 3, p.383
Words of 'Abdu'l-Bahá, p.182 : *Promulgation of Universal Peace*, p.386

Chapter 35:
Words of 'Abdu'l-Bahá, p.184 : *Chosen Highway*, p.259

Bibliography

Stories of Bahá'u'lláh compiled by 'Ali-Akbar Furutan (UK, George Ronald 1986)

The Revelation of Bahá'u'lláh Vol. 1-4 by Adib Taherzadeh (UK, George Ronald 1975, 1977, 1983, 1988)

Bahá'u'lláh: The King of Glory by H.M. Balyuzi (UK, George Ronald 1980)

The Promulgation of Universal Peace by 'Abdu'l-Bahá (USA, Bahá'í Publishing Trust 1982)

God Passes By by Shoghi Effendi (USA, Bahá'í Publishing Trust 1979)

Bahá'í Holy Places at the World Centre (Haifa, Bahá'í World Centre 1968)

Ṭáhirih the Pure by Martha Root (USA, Kalimat 1981)

Bahá'u'lláh and the New Era by J.E. Esslemont (UK, Bahá'í Publishing Trust 1974)

The Chosen Highway by Lady Blomfield (USA, Bahá'í Publishing Trust 1975)

Bahá'u'lláh by H.M. Balyuzi (UK, George Ronald 1974)

Christ and Bahá'u'lláh by George Townshend (UK, George Ronald 1971)

Stories from The Delight of Hearts by Hájí Mírzá Haydar-'Alí translated by A.Q. Faizi (USA, Kalimat 1980)

The Dawnbreakers by Nabíl-i-A'ẓam translated by Shoghi Effendi (USA, Bahá'í Publishing Trust 1974)

Some Answered Questions by 'Abdu'l-Bahá, collected and translated by Laura Clifford Barney (USA, Bahá'í Publishing Trust 1987)

The Summons of the Lord of Hosts - Tablets of Bahá'u'lláh (Australia, Bahá'í Publishing Trust, 2002)

The Master in 'Akká by Myron Phelps (USA, Kalimat 1985)

A Guide to Pronunciation

Taken from *The Dawnbreakers*, p. 673

t̲h̲	pronounced as	s		
d̲h̲	pronounced as	z		
z̲h̲	pronounced as	j		
ṣ	pronounced as	s		
ḍ	pronounced as	z		
ṭ	pronounced as	t		
ẓ	pronounced as	z		
a	as	a	in	account
á	as	a	in	arm
i	as	e	in	best
í	as	ee	in	meet
u	as	o	in	short
ú	as	oo	in	moon
aw	as	ow	in	mown

Shirin Sabri is a poet and writer, currently working as a teacher of History and English at Townshend International School. Her poems have been published in *The Bahá'í World*, in *Canadian Bahá'í Studies* monographs, *Imago* and *Poetry Australia*. In an earlier collaboration with Sue Podger, the illustrator of this book, she wrote the children's fantasy novel, *The Pinckelhoffer Mice*.

Sue Podger is descended from the early Dutch settlers of the Cape of Good Hope, South Africa. She is the first of this people to become a Bahá'í. She was trained at the Michaelis School of Fine Art in Cape Town. An accomplished watercolourist, she uses a range of styles to portray a sensitive and accurate picture of the years when Bahá'u'lláh was amongst us.

Massoud Tahzib is a gifted designer of books. His settings for these beautiful stories come from a deeply felt Bahá'í heritage.